Texas
Bed
&
Breakfast
Cookbook

Enjoy!
Virginia

Texas Bed & Breakfast Cookbook

First Edition

Design: Lisa Bachar
Cover location: The Lodges at Lost Maples, Vanderpool, Texas
Cover photos: Laurence Parent Photography (top); StockFood/Prost (bottom)
Author photo: Ted Spring Photography
Editing: Melissa Craven & Susan Larson

ISBN 1-889593-07-9

Printed in China

3D Press, Inc.
4340 E. Kentucky Ave., Suite 446
Denver, CO 80246
303-300-4484 (phone)
303-300-4494 (fax)
info@3dpress.net (email)

888-456-3607 (order toll-free)
www.3dpress.net

We dedicate this cookbook
to all of the warm-hearted,
hard-working Texas bed &
breakfast owners, innkeepers and
chefs, who took time from their
busy schedules to generously
share their favorite recipes.

Thanks, y'all!

Carol and Erin

Acknowledgements

Creating this cookbook involved contributions from many people. We owe a great deal of gratitude to friends, family members and business colleagues for their inspiration, time, talents, enthusiasm and support. Thanks to:

Dave Rich, for believing in our project, and his months of hard work, expertise and encouragement.

Melissa Craven, for her endless hours of researching and editing.

Susan Larson and Holly Bell, for their sharp editorial eyes.

Lisa Bachar, for her creative input and cover design.

Jack and Susan Baker, for generously sharing their beautiful kitchen for the author photo-shoot and their participation in recipe taste-testing.

Scott Leonard, for his willingness to taste-test innumerable recipes and offer helpful culinary comments and suggestions along the way.

Rod Faino, for enthusiastically eating yet one more egg dish or stack of pancakes for dinner – with never a complaint.

Moss Haven Elementary School colleagues in Richardson, Texas, for their recipe taste-testing enthusiasm, interest and support.

Jamie and Grover McMains, owners/innkeepers of the Texas White House in Fort Worth, as well as numerous other Historic Accommodations of Texas (www.hat.org/800-HAT-0368) property owners, for their contributions and invaluable help.

The *Texas Bed & Breakfast Cookbook* is the third book in the Bed & Breakfast Cookbook Series™, a series of state-by-state bed & breakfast cookbooks originally created and published by Carol Faino and Doreen Hazledine.

Table of Contents

Introduction

The *Texas Bed & Breakfast Cookbook* is the newest addition to our state-by-state Bed & Breakfast Cookbook Series. We were delighted with the opportunity to do a book for a state with such rich cultural history, expansive and varied geographical regions, and where we had the pleasure of living for more than ten years. Seventy fascinating bed and breakfasts, guest ranches, hotels and country inns throughout the state of Texas were chosen to be a part of this latest offering.

Generous and gracious Texas innkeepers, owners and chefs have shared 150 of their most delicious and prized recipes for your enjoyment. We tested the recipes in our home kitchens and edited them for ease and clarity for the everyday cook. You can be assured of successful and consistent results, and delight in compliments from family and friends.

In addition to being a great recipe collection, this book may also be used to seek out distinctive and special places to visit. Imagine staying in a beautifully preserved, historic Victorian mansion, or perhaps lounging in a rustic log cabin. Picture yourself relaxing in a quiet, cozy, seaside cottage, or having a thrilling adventure at a working ranch. The choice is yours!

Each bed and breakfast experience is unique because each inn has its own personality, and each innkeeper has his/her own individual qualities that bring charm and excitement to the occasion. Being pampered with a tasty, beautifully presented, bountiful breakfast is a wonderful way to greet the new day.

So whether you try these tempting recipes at home, or enjoy them at one of the many fine, featured bed and breakfasts in the *Texas Bed & Breakfast Cookbook*, we wish you the very best in culinary experiences. Here's to happy traveling and great adventures throughout the Lone Star State!

Enjoy making memories,

Carol & Erin

Breads, Muffins, Biscuits & Granola

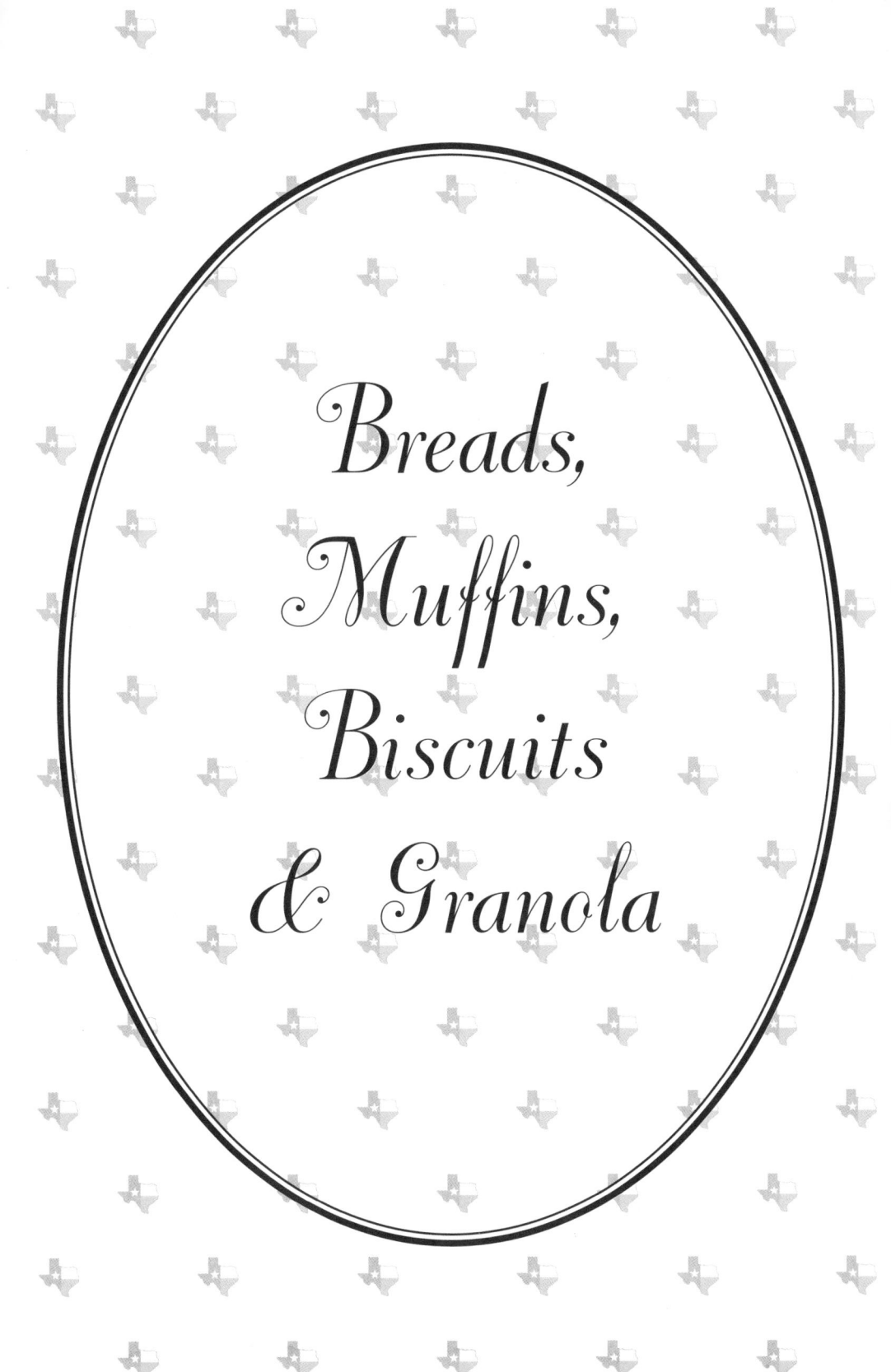

Breads,
Muffins,
Biscuits
& Granola

Captain's House on the Lake

The Captain's House on the Lake Bed & Breakfast and 1909 Guesthouse is "where pampering and excellent service are a way of life." Sip away the evening with some of Ms. Julia's famous peach tea before you visit the historic square and "do the town." In the morning, step outside and take in the beautiful lake view while you enjoy breakfast on the balcony or patio.

The Captain's House was rated as one of the "Five Most Romantic Spots in Texas" by *AAA Travel* magazine.

INNKEEPERS:	Bob & Julia Pannell
ADDRESS:	123 West Doyle Street
	Granbury, Texas 76048
TELEPHONE:	(817) 579-6664
E-MAIL:	captain@itexas.net
WEBSITE:	www.captainshouse.info
ROOMS:	1 Room; 2 Suites; 2 Guesthouses; Private baths
CHILDREN:	Children age 14 and older are welcome
ANIMALS:	Not allowed; Resident pet
HANDICAPPED:	Not handicapped accessible
DIETARY NEEDS:	Will accommodate guests' special dietary needs

Julia's Heavenly Cinnamon Bread with Fruit Topping

Makes 8 Servings

1   (18-ounce) box cinnamon streusel quick bread mix
Cooking oil (amount according to bread mix directions)
Eggs (amount according to bread mix directions)
1   cup chopped nuts, divided
1   stick (½ cup) butter, divided
4   green apples (such as Granny Smith), diced or thinly sliced
¼   cup raisins (optional)
Cinnamon, to taste
8   large or 16 small strawberries, diced or thinly sliced
4   bananas, cut into thick slices
¼   cup honey
1   large naval orange, cut into 16 bite-size chunks, for garnish
Powdered sugar, for garnish (optional)

Preheat oven to temperature called for by bread mix. Grease the bottom of a 9x5-inch loaf pan. Prepare bread mix batter according to mix directions. Spoon ½ of batter into loaf pan. Sprinkle with ½ of streusel topping from bread mix and ½ cup nuts. Spoon remaining batter on top. Sprinkle with remaining streusel and remaining nuts. Bake according to mix directions. When done, cool in pan for 15 minutes, then turn out onto a wire rack.

While the bread is cooling, melt ½ stick of butter in a large nonstick skillet over medium heat. Add the apples, coating with butter and browning lightly. Add the raisins. Sprinkle with cinnamon. Remove from heat; cover to keep warm. In another nonstick skillet, melt remaining ½ stick of butter. Add strawberries and bananas; cook lightly (do not overcook). During the last minute of cooking, dribble with the honey and turn twice.

To serve, cut warm bread into 8 slices. Place 1 slice on each plate. Spoon a little apple mixture onto each slice. Top with bananas and strawberries. Garnish with 2 orange chunks. Sprinkle with powdered sugar, if desired.

The Cotton Palace

Located in a 1910 Arts and Crafts-style house, the Cotton Palace Bed & Breakfast has been completely renovated to showcase the exquisite woodwork and design of Roy Elspeth Lane, Waco's premier architect. The Cotton Palace is a retreat – whether staying for business or pleasure.

"A step away from the everyday world. A place of beauty, peaceful rest and sumptuous food." ~ Guest, The Cotton Palace

INNKEEPERS:	Becky Hodges and Dutch & Betty Schroeder
ADDRESS:	1910 Austin Avenue
	Waco, Texas 76701
TELEPHONE:	(254) 753-7294; (877) 632-2312
E-MAIL:	cotnpalace@aol.com
WEBSITE:	www.thecottonpalace.com
ROOMS:	4 Rooms; 2 Suites; 1 Cottage; Private baths
CHILDREN:	Children age 12 and older welcome
ANIMALS:	Not allowed
HANDICAPPED:	Not handicapped accessible
DIETARY NEEDS:	Will accommodate guests' special dietary needs

Glazed Cream Cheese Bread

Makes 4 Loaves

Plan ahead – the dough needs to chill overnight before making and baking the bread. This bread freezes well!

1	cup sour cream
½	cup plus ¾ cup sugar
1	teaspoon plus ⅛ teaspoon salt
1	stick (½ cup) butter, melted
2	packages (5 teaspoons) active dry yeast
½	cup warm water (105-115°F)
2	eggs, beaten plus 1 egg, beaten
4	cups flour
2	(8-ounce) packages cream cheese, room temperature
2	teaspoons plus 1 teaspoon vanilla extract
2	cups powdered sugar
¼	cup milk

Heat sour cream in a small saucepan over low heat. Stir in ½ cup sugar, 1 teaspoon salt and butter. Remove from heat and let cool to lukewarm. Sprinkle yeast over warm water in a large mixing bowl; stir to dissolve. Add sour cream mixture, 2 beaten eggs and flour; mix well. Tightly cover dough and chill overnight.

The next day, divide dough into 4 equal portions. On a well-floured surface, roll each portion into a 12x18-inch rectangle. Combine cream cheese, ¾ cup sugar, 1 beaten egg, ⅛ teaspoon salt and 2 teaspoons of vanilla; mix until smooth. Spread ¼ of the cream cheese filling over each rectangle of dough. Beginning at long edge, roll up, jelly-roll style. Pinch seam to seal; tuck ends under. Place rolls, seam-side-down, on greased baking sheets. Cut slits about ⅔ of the way through the dough at 2-inch intervals. Cover and let rise in a warm place (80-85°F) for about 1 hour, or until doubled in size.

Preheat oven to 375°F. Bake for 12-15 minutes. While bread is baking, make a glaze by combining 1 teaspoon vanilla, powdered sugar and milk. Blend until smooth. Spread glaze over warm loaves.

BlissWood

The BlissWood Bed & Breakfast is conveniently located in Cat Spring, approximately 60 miles west of Houston. The area around the inn is rich in Texas historical attractions. Guests enjoy exploring the cultural attractions and numerous antique shops in the nearby communities, guided horseback rides, bass fishing, trap shooting, archery and golf.

The Writer's Cabin is a secluded one-bedroom house hidden back amongst the oaks. If you need to truly get away, this is a place of perfect seclusion.

INNKEEPERS:	Carol Davis
ADDRESS:	13300 Lehmann Legacy Lane
	Cat Spring, Texas 78933
TELEPHONE:	(713) 301-3235; (800) 753-3376
E-MAIL:	carol@blisswood.net
WEBSITE:	www.blisswood.net
ROOMS:	9 Rooms; Private baths
CHILDREN:	Call ahead
ANIMALS:	Call ahead; Resident dogs
HANDICAPPED:	Handicapped accessible
DIETARY NEEDS:	Will accommodate guests' special dietary needs

Blueberry Cornbread Mini-Loaves

Makes 3 Small Loaves

"Wrap and store these loaves overnight – they're actually tastier the day after baking." – Innkeeper, BlissWood Bed & Breakfast

1½	cups flour
1½	cups yellow cornmeal
¾	cup sugar
1	tablespoon baking powder
½	teaspoon salt
½	teaspoon plus 1 teaspoon finely grated lemon zest
2	eggs, beaten
1¼	cups milk
½	teaspoon vanilla extract
¼	cup vegetable oil (such as canola)
1	cup fresh blueberries (or substitute frozen blueberries)
¾	cup plus 1 tablespoon sifted powdered sugar
2	teaspoons lemon juice

Water or milk (about 2-3 teaspoons)

1	stick (½ cup) butter, room temperature

Preheat oven to 350°F. Grease bottoms and ½ inch up the sides of 3 small 5x3-inch loaf pans. In a large bowl, combine flour, cornmeal, sugar, baking powder, salt and ½ teaspoon lemon zest. Make a well in center of dry ingredients. In another bowl, combine eggs, milk, vanilla and oil; add to dry ingredients and stir just until moistened. Fold in blueberries. Spoon batter into pans. Bake for 35-40 minutes, or until a toothpick inserted in the center comes out clean. Cool in pans on wire racks for 10 minutes. Remove from pans. Cool completely. Wrap loaves tightly and store overnight.

The next day, make a lemon glaze by combining ¾ cup powdered sugar, lemon juice and enough water or milk to reach a drizzling consistency. Make a lemon butter by combining butter, 1 tablespoon powdered sugar and 1 teaspoon lemon zest. Drizzle the loaves with the lemon glaze and serve with lemon butter.

Gruene Apple

At the end of a tree-lined lane, on a bluff overlooking the Guadalupe River, you will find the Gruene Apple Bed & Breakfast. With its magnificent limestone exterior, expansive porches and soaring 22-foot-high entrance hall, the Gruene Apple offers a world of unsurpassed elegance and hospitality.

Settle into a wingback swivel chair in the media room to watch a movie on the 12-foot-wide screen. Or, take a refreshing dip in the natural stone swimming pool and hot tub.

INNKEEPERS:	Ki, Lloyd & Linda Kleypas
ADDRESS:	1235 Gruene Road
	New Braunfels, Texas 78130
TELEPHONE:	(830) 643-1234
E-MAIL:	grueneappl@aol.com
WEBSITE:	www.grueneapple.com
ROOMS:	14 Rooms; Private baths
CHILDREN:	Children age 12 and older welcome
ANIMALS:	Not allowed; Resident cats
HANDICAPPED:	Handicapped accessible
DIETARY NEEDS:	Will accommodate guests' special dietary needs

Pumpkin Coconut Bread

Makes 1 Loaf

2	eggs
1	cup sugar
¾	cup vegetable oil
1½	cups flour
1	teaspoon baking powder
1	teaspoon baking soda
½	teaspoon salt
½	teaspoon nutmeg
½	teaspoon ground ginger
½	teaspoon cinnamon
1	(3½-ounce) package instant coconut cream pudding mix
1	cup canned or cooked mashed pumpkin
½	cup chopped pecans

Preheat oven to 350°F. Spray a 9x5-inch loaf pan with nonstick cooking spray. Beat together eggs, sugar and oil in a large bowl. Combine flour, baking powder, baking soda, salt, nutmeg, ginger, cinnamon and pudding mix in a medium bowl. Add dry ingredients to egg mixture. Beat on low speed with a mixer, just until combined. Stir in pumpkin and pecans. Spoon batter into prepared pan.

Bake for 60 minutes, or until a toothpick inserted in the center comes out clean. Cool in pan for 10 minutes. Remove loaf from pan. Cool loaf completely on a wire rack.

Casa de Siesta

The Casa de Siesta Bed & Breakfast is located on South Padre Island, a coastal resort town on the Gulf of Mexico with five miles of seashore fun, shopping, dining and water activities. The island, bordered by the Laguna Madre bay, is also ecologically significant with 34 miles of sand dunes, water birds, shrimp and the best deep-sea fishing in Texas.

All the building materials and decor of Casa de Siesta are representative of Mexican, North American and Anglo cultures of the Southwest.

INNKEEPERS:	Ron & Lynn Speier
ADDRESS:	4610 Padre Boulevard
	South Padre Island, Texas 78597
TELEPHONE:	(956) 761-5656
E-MAIL:	reservations@casadesiesta.com
WEBSITE:	www.casadesiesta.com
ROOMS:	12 Rooms; Private baths
CHILDREN:	Children age 12 and older welcome
ANIMALS:	Welcome
HANDICAPPED:	Handicapped accessible
DIETARY NEEDS:	Will accommodate guests' special dietary needs

Banana Applesauce Bread

Makes 2 Loaves

"Save your overripe bananas for this bread (they will last for a few more days in the refrigerator, or they can also be frozen, if you are not quite ready to make this delicious bread)." ~ Innkeeper, Casa de Siesta Bed & Breakfast

1   stick (½ cup) butter, room temperature
1½   cups sugar
2   eggs
3-4   very ripe bananas, chopped into small pieces (about 2 cups)
½   cup applesauce
2   cups flour
1   teaspoon baking soda
¼   teaspoon salt
1   cup chopped walnuts

Preheat oven to 325°F. Grease and flour two 9x5-inch loaf pans. Cream together butter and sugar in a large bowl. Add eggs, bananas and applesauce; beat on low speed with a mixer until well combined. Sift together flour, baking soda and salt; add to wet ingredients and mix well. Stir in nuts. Divide mixture between loaf pans (pans will be slightly less than ½-full).

Bake for 50-55 minutes, or until a toothpick inserted in the center comes out clean. Let loaves cool in the pans on a wire rack for 10 minutes. Turn loaves out. Bread may be served warm, or cooled completely for later use. Slice and serve on a doily-lined plate.

River Run

Nestled above the Guadalupe River in the heart of Kerrville, the River Run Bed & Breakfast Inn takes you back to an earlier age, when people actually took time to sit on the front porch and visit with family and friends. Built of native stone, with a high, sloping tin roof, the inn reflects the spirit of German-style Hill Country architecture.

A short walk from the front porch will take you to the antique stores of Water Street as well as several excellent restaurants.

INNKEEPERS:	Ron & Jean Williamson
ADDRESS:	120 Francisco Lemos Street
	Kerrville, Texas 78028
TELEPHONE:	(830) 896-8353; (800) 460-7170
E-MAIL:	riverrun@ktc.com
WEBSITE:	www.riverrunbb.com
ROOMS:	4 Rooms; 2 Suites; Private baths
CHILDREN:	Children age 17 and older welcome
ANIMALS:	Not allowed
HANDICAPPED:	Handicapped accessible; 1 room
DIETARY NEEDS:	Will accommodate guests' special dietary needs

The Dutchman's Date Loaf

Makes 10 Servings

"This recipe is an updated version of a trail drivers' favorite that cowboys would bribe their trail cook to prepare. There is a tale that one outfit went so far as to promise their cook, known only as the Dutchman, a night on the town and a bottle of the finest champagne if he would only fix the quick bread in his famous Dutch oven. As it turned out, the cook took them up on the offer, but the cowboys reneged on their promise once they got to Dodge City. The cook then quit the outfit and signed up with a restaurant in town. After the cowboys finally sobered up from their celebrating in the town's saloons, they realized what a big mistake they had made. It took a new pony, a saddle and a new hat to convince the cook to return to their outfit. In the Old West, good cooks were hard to come by!" ~ Innkeeper, River Run Bed & Breakfast Inn

1½	cups milk
1	cup old-fashioned rolled oats (not quick-cooking oats)
1	cup chopped dates
2	cups baking mix (such as Bisquick)
⅔	cup sugar
⅓	cup packed brown sugar
½	cup chopped walnuts
1	large egg
⅓	cup applesauce
⅓	cup canola oil

Preheat oven to 325°F. Grease and flour a 12-cup Bundt pan. Put milk in a 2-cup glass measuring cup; heat in microwave oven until almost simmering. Put oats and dates in a medium bowl; stir in the hot milk. Cool to room temperature.

Combine baking mix, sugar, brown sugar and walnuts in a large bowl. Make a well in the center; set aside. Beat egg, applesauce and oil into cooled oat mixture; add to dry ingredients and stir until well combined. Pour batter into pan. Bake for 45-50 minutes, or until top is crusty and golden. Cool on a wire rack for 10 minutes. Remove loaf from pan and cool on the rack for 20 minutes more. Slice and enjoy.

Amelia's Place

A melia's Place is a welcoming, three-story, warehouse-style loft "deep in the heart of downtown Dallas." Enjoy good conversation, play Amelia's piano, read, play Scrabble or just relax. A block from the library and city hall, and two blocks from the original Neiman-Marcus and the convention center, the Dart Trolley-Bus stops at Amelia's corner every 10 minutes.

"Her breakfasts are so good and so big you can skip lunch." ~ Guest, Amelia's Place Bed & Breakfast

INNKEEPERS:	Amelia Core Jenkins
ADDRESS:	1775 Young Street
	Dallas, Texas 75201
TELEPHONE:	(214) 651-1775; (888) 651-1775
E-MAIL:	ameliaj@flash.net
WEBSITE:	www.ameliasplace.com
ROOMS:	6 Rooms; Private & shared baths
CHILDREN:	Children age 14 and older welcome
ANIMALS:	Not allowed
HANDICAPPED:	Not handicapped accessible
DIETARY NEEDS:	Will accommodate guests' special dietary needs

Mexican Cornbread

Makes 8 to 9 Servings

"This is a meal in a skillet; you only need to add a green salad." ~ Innkeeper, Amelia's Place Bed & Breakfast

1	cup yellow cornmeal
½	cup self-rising flour
1	teaspoon salt
½	teaspoon baking soda
1	(14¾-ounce) can cream-style corn
1	large onion, chopped
½	cup chopped green bell pepper
½	cup finely chopped celery
1¼	cups finely chopped hot-flavored smoked sausage (about 12-inches)
2	eggs
1	cup milk
¼	cup vegetable oil

Preheat oven to 400°F. Spray a 9x9-inch baking pan or a 9-inch cast-iron skillet with nonstick cooking spray. Sift together cornmeal, flour, salt and baking soda into a large bowl. Add corn, onion, bell pepper, celery and sausage. In a small bowl, lightly beat eggs, milk and oil; add to the cornmeal mixture and stir just until moistened.

Bake for 50-60 minutes, or until a toothpick inserted in the center comes out clean. Let cornbread cool on a wire rack for 15-20 minutes before serving. Serve warm.

Note: For a spicier cornbread, add a small can of taco sauce, chopped jalapeño peppers or a small can of chopped green chiles to the batter before baking.

Austin's Wildflower Inn

Each room at Austin's Wildflower Inn is furnished with antiques, and has been carefully prepared, awaiting your arrival. Guests awaken to the aroma of fresh-brewed coffee and home-baked breads and muffins. A full buffet breakfast is served in the elegant dining room or on the deck.

Innkeeper Kay Jackson is a descendent of David G. Burnet, President of the Republic of Texas. Her grandfather, David Burnet Walker, was a two-term Flotorial Representative of the Texas House of Representatives.

INNKEEPERS:	Kay Jackson & Claudean Schultz
ADDRESS:	1200 West 22½ Street
	Austin, Texas 78705
TELEPHONE:	(512) 477-9639
E-MAIL:	kjackson@austinswildflowerinn.com
WEBSITE:	www.austinswildflowerinn.com
ROOMS:	3 Rooms; Private baths
CHILDREN:	Call ahead
ANIMALS:	Not allowed
HANDICAPPED:	Not handicapped accessible
DIETARY NEEDS:	Call ahead

Cheddar Zucchini Wedges

Makes 6 to 8 Servings

Enjoy this hearty, savory bread for breakfast, or as an accompaniment for chicken or other meat at dinner. This is a great recipe to try when the Farmers' Markets are abundant with zucchini.

½	stick (¼ cup) butter
1	medium onion, chopped
2½	cups baking mix (such as Bisquick)
1	tablespoon minced fresh parsley
½	teaspoon dried basil
½	teaspoon dried thyme
3	eggs, beaten
¼	cup milk
1½	cups grated zucchini (about 2 small zucchini)
1	cup (4 ounces) grated cheddar cheese
¾	cup chopped toasted almonds*

Preheat oven to 400°F. Spray a 9- or 10-inch round baking pan or pie pan with nonstick cooking spray. Melt butter in a skillet over medium-low heat. Add onion; cook until translucent and tender.

Combine baking mix, parsley, basil and thyme in a large bowl. Stir in cooked onion. Add beaten eggs and milk; stir just until combined. Gently fold in zucchini, cheese and almonds. Transfer mixture to the baking pan.

Bake for 25-30 minutes, or until a toothpick inserted in the center comes out clean. Let stand for about 5 minutes. Cut into wedges and serve.

*To toast the almonds: Place a small dry skillet over medium heat. Add the nuts. Stir the nuts frequently until a good color and aroma are achieved (this only takes a few minutes). Pour the almonds out onto a plate to cool; spread into a thin layer to prevent any further browning.

Gruene Mansion Inn

The Gruene Mansion Inn has captured the drama and historical flair of Henry D. Gruene's Victorian home in this award-winning bed and breakfast. Not only is the property listed on the National Register of Historic Places, but it is also designated a Texas Historic Landmark.

Such notable musicians as Jerry Jeff Walker, Lyle Lovett, Willie Nelson, the Dixie Chicks and George Strait have all held center stage at the adjacent Gruene Hall, "the oldest dance hall in Texas."

INNKEEPERS:	Cecil & Judi Eager
ADDRESS:	1275 Gruene Road
	New Braunfels, Texas 78130
TELEPHONE:	(830) 629-2641
E-MAIL:	frontdesk@gruenemansioninn.com
WEBSITE:	www.gruenemansioninn.com
ROOMS:	30 Rooms; 12 Suites; 1 Cottage; Private baths
CHILDREN:	Welcome
ANIMALS:	Not allowed
HANDICAPPED:	Handicapped accessible
DIETARY NEEDS:	Will accommodate guests' special dietary needs

White Chocolate Apricot Muffins

Makes 12 Muffins

"These flavorful muffins are good with or without the crystallized ginger." ~
Innkeeper, Gruene Mansion Inn

1¼	cups flour
½	cup plus 2 tablespoons sugar
1½	teaspoons baking powder
½	teaspoon salt
1	tablespoon minced crystallized ginger
2	(1-ounce) squares white baking chocolate, finely chopped
¾	cup 1% milk
3	tablespoons butter, melted
1	large egg, lightly beaten
½	cup apricot preserves

Preheat oven to 400°F. Spray 12 muffin cups with nonstick cooking spray.
Combine flour, ½ cup sugar, baking powder, salt, crystallized ginger and
chopped white chocolate in a large bowl. Make a well in the center.
Combine milk, melted butter and egg in a small bowl; add to the dry
ingredients and stir until just combined.

Spoon 1 tablespoon of batter into each muffin cup. Put about 1¼ teaspoons
of apricot preserves in the center of the batter in each muffin cup. Top with
1 tablespoon of batter. Sprinkle each muffin with ½ teaspoon sugar. Bake
for 20-22 minutes. Cool for 5 minutes in the muffin pan on a wire rack.
Remove from pan. Serve warm, or cool for later use.

Munzesheimer Manor

At the Munzesheimer Manor, you can sip lemonade on the wrap-around porches, sleep in custom Victorian nightgowns and nightshirts, bathe in a turn-of-the-century, claw-foot tub (with your own rubber ducky) or treat yourself to a bubble-bath with therapeutic bath salts.

The Engineer's Room is decorated in a railroad theme, complete with the "dead man's clutch," large caboose lamp and other relics of Mineola's historic connection to the railroad, which dates back to 1873.

INNKEEPERS:	Bob & Sherry Murray
ADDRESS:	202 North Newsom
	Mineola, Texas 75773
TELEPHONE:	(903) 569-6634
E-MAIL:	innkeeper@munzesheimer.com
WEBSITE:	www.munzesheimer.com
ROOMS:	4 Rooms; 3 Cottages; Private baths
CHILDREN:	Welcome; Call ahead
ANIMALS:	Not allowed; Resident dog
HANDICAPPED:	Call ahead
DIETARY NEEDS:	Will accommodate guests' special dietary needs

Morning Glory Mini-Muffins

Makes 4 Dozen Mini-Muffins

"This batter can be made in advance and frozen in the muffin pans. Thaw overnight in the refrigerator when ready to use." ~ Innkeeper, Munzesheimer Manor Bed & Breakfast

2	cups flour
1	cup sugar
2	teaspoons baking soda
2	teaspoons cinnamon
1	apple, peeled, cored and grated —OR 3/4 C DRAINED CRUSHED PINEAPPLE
½	cup raisins
½	cup shredded coconut
½	cup chopped pecans
1	cup grated carrot
3	eggs
½	cup vegetable oil
1	stick (½ cup) butter, melted
2	teaspoons vanilla extract

Preheat oven to 350°F. Spray mini-muffin cups with nonstick cooking spray. In a large bowl, sift together flour, sugar, baking soda and cinnamon. Add grated apple, raisins, coconut, pecans and grated carrot. Mix thoroughly, until mixture resembles a coarse meal.

In a medium bowl, beat eggs with a whisk. Add oil, butter and vanilla; whisk to blend. Add wet ingredients to dry ingredients; stir just until combined. Spoon batter into muffin cups. (At this point, the batter can be covered and frozen.) Bake for 10-12 minutes, or until done. Cool for 5 minutes before removing muffins from muffin pans. Serve warm.

Wisteria Hideaway

G uests are invited to a full breakfast at Wisteria Hideaway Bed & Breakfast. Breakfast meats are custom processed, providing a flavorful accompaniment to dishes that vary from creamy scrambled eggs and frittatas to spicy egg casseroles. Buttermilk biscuits baked to a tender crust in an iron skillet, or sweet potato muffins go nicely with the inn's homemade jellies.

The dining room features original wall coverings and full-length windows.

INNKEEPERS:	Ron & Brenda A. Cole
ADDRESS:	3458 Ted Trout Drive
	Lufkin, Texas 75904
TELEPHONE:	(936) 875-2914
E-MAIL:	info@wisteriahideaway.com
WEBSITE:	www.wisteriahideaway.com
ROOMS:	2 Rooms; 1 Suite; Private baths
CHILDREN:	Welcome
ANIMALS:	Not allowed; Resident outdoor cat
HANDICAPPED:	Handicapped accessible
DIETARY NEEDS:	Will accommodate guests' special dietary needs

Sweet Potato Muffins

Makes 12 Muffins

"For these muffins, I bake sweet potatoes, then cool and freeze them until ready to use. I feel they have better flavor than boiled sweet potatoes." ~ Innkeeper, Wisteria Hideaway Bed & Breakfast

1½   cups flour
¾   cup sugar
¾   teaspoon baking powder
½   teaspoon baking soda
½   teaspoon cinnamon
½   teaspoon salt
¼   cup vegetable oil
¼   cup water
2   eggs, slightly beaten
¾   cup cooked, mashed sweet potato (may also used drained canned sweet potatoes)

Preheat oven to 400°F. Spray 12 muffin cups with nonstick cooking spray. Combine flour, sugar, baking powder, baking soda, cinnamon and salt in a large bowl. Combine oil, water, eggs and sweet potatoes in another bowl. Add wet ingredients to dry ingredients; stir just until moistened. Spoon batter into muffin cups.

Bake for 20 minutes, or until a toothpick inserted in the center comes out clean. Cool in pans on a wire rack for 5 minutes. Serve warm.

Rockin River Inn

The Rockin River Inn is surrounded by Hill Country native landscapes that display a Texas wildflower show in the spring and a spectacular changing of the leaves in the fall. A full gourmet breakfast includes farm-raised eggs and home-baked pastries. The inn has a swimming pool and offers hunting packages and bike trail maps.

The Rockin River Inn is constructed of long-leaf pine floors, 20-inch-thick walls and hammered brass door hardware, and boasts a native-stone fireplace.

INNKEEPERS:	Betty & Ken Wardlaw
ADDRESS:	106 Skyline Road
	Center Point, Texas 78010
TELEPHONE:	(830) 634-7043; (866) 424-0576
E-MAIL:	relax@rockinriverinn.com
WEBSITE:	www.rockinriverinn.com
ROOMS:	3 Rooms; 1 Suite; Private baths
CHILDREN:	Welcome
ANIMALS:	Not allowed; Resident dog
HANDICAPPED:	Not handicapped accessible
DIETARY NEEDS:	Will accommodate guests' special dietary needs

Fredericksburg Peach Muffins

Makes 12 Muffins

"I created this muffin recipe to take advantage of the big, juicy peaches grown all around Fredericksburg and Stonewall. When the short summer peach season is over, you can substitute good quality frozen peaches – and only those who live in the Hill Country will know the difference." ~ Innkeeper, Rockin River Inn

1	cup flour
1	teaspoon baking powder
½	teaspoon baking soda
¼	teaspoon salt
2	eggs
1	cup premium whole milk yogurt (do not use low-fat or non-fat)
¾	cup packed brown sugar
1	cup quick-cooking or old-fashioned rolled oats
⅓	cup butter, melted
½	teaspoon lemon extract
1	teaspoon grated lemon zest
1	cup chopped (½-inch cubes), peeled fresh or frozen peaches
¾	cup finely chopped walnuts

Preheat oven to 350°F. Spray 12 muffin cups with nonstick cooking spray. Combine flour, baking powder, baking soda and salt in a medium bowl; make a well in the center.

In another bowl, combine eggs, yogurt, brown sugar, oats, melted butter, lemon extract and lemon zest; add to dry ingredients and stir just until moistened. Add peaches and walnuts; stir gently just until combined. Fill muffin cups ¾-full.

Bake for 20-22 minutes on center rack of oven, or until the center of each muffin springs back when lightly pressed. Cool for 5 minutes in muffin cups before removing muffins to a wire rack.

Austin's Wildflower Inn

T hroughout Austin's Wildflower Inn you will see beautiful original oak hardwood floors, antique furniture in every room, handmade quilts and elegant lace curtains. A spacious porch with comfortable chairs graces the front of the house. It is a perfect spot for enjoying the beautiful gardens.

The impressive bi-level deck in the backyard garden is the ideal place for a special breakfast. Spend the day enjoying Austin, then retire to the shaded side yard to sip iced tea.

INNKEEPERS:	Kay Jackson & Claudean Schultz
ADDRESS:	1200 West 22½ Street
	Austin, Texas 78705
TELEPHONE:	(512) 477-9639
E-MAIL:	kjackson@austinswildflowerinn.com
WEBSITE:	www.austinswildflowerinn.com
ROOMS:	3 Rooms; Private baths
CHILDREN:	Call ahead
ANIMALS:	Not allowed
HANDICAPPED:	Not handicapped accessible
DIETARY NEEDS:	Call ahead

Pumpkin Streusel Muffins

Makes 24 Muffins

These muffins are not too sweet – just right, especially with the streusel topping.

3½   cups flour
1   cup packed brown sugar
1   tablespoon plus 1 teaspoon baking powder
1½   teaspoons cinnamon
1   teaspoon salt
1   teaspoon nutmeg
1¼   cups cooked or canned pumpkin purée
2   eggs, beaten
1   cup milk
⅔   cup vegetable oil
2   (3-ounce) packages cream cheese, cut into 24 small chunks
Streusel topping (recipe follows)

Preheat oven to 375°F. Line 24 muffin cups with paper muffin liners. Sift together flour, brown sugar, baking powder, cinnamon, salt and nutmeg into a large bowl; set aside. Whisk together pumpkin, eggs, milk and oil. Add dry ingredients to wet ingredients; stir until moistened and combined.

Fill muffin cups ½-full. Put 1 cream cheese chunk in center of batter in each cup; top with remaining batter. Sprinkle streusel topping over batter in muffin cups. Bake for 20-22 minutes. Cool on a wire rack. Refrigerate leftover muffins.

Streusel topping:
½   cup packed brown sugar
1   teaspoon cinnamon
2   tablespoons butter, melted
½   cup chopped walnuts

Combine brown sugar, cinnamon and butter in a small mixing bowl. Stir in walnuts.

The Branscombe

Wrap yourself in a quilt and old-time charm at the Branscombe. Situated in the historic Irish Town district of Corpus Christi, the Branscombe is within blocks of the city's tourist activities, including Selena Auditorium, Art Museum of South Texas, Bayfront Plaza, Columbus Ships, Heritage Park and the Science Museum, to name a few.

The Branscombe is a duplex, so guests have use of the entire north side, including a living room, kitchen and access to the lovely patio and garden.

INNKEEPERS:	Beverly Randolph
ADDRESS:	1319 North Chaparral
	Corpus Christi, Texas 78401
TELEPHONE:	(361) 888-4184
E-MAIL:	innkeeper@thebranscombe.com
WEBSITE:	www.thebranscombe.com
ROOMS:	1 Suite; Private bath
CHILDREN:	Not allowed
ANIMALS:	Not allowed; Resident outdoor cats
HANDICAPPED:	Not handicapped accessible
DIETARY NEEDS:	Will accommodate guests' special dietary needs

Bev's "Raved-About" Oat Bran Muffins

Make 6 "Texas-size" Muffins or 12 Regular Muffins

1   (8.1-ounce) package muffin mix (such as Martha White or Jiffy), flavor of choice
1   cup oat bran hot cereal (such as Hodgson Mill)
½   cup packed dark brown sugar
1   cup chopped pecans
½   cup Sun-Maid Goldens & Cherries (golden raisins and tart cherries)
2   eggs
½   cup milk
Orange juice (about ½ cup)
Butter, for serving

Preheat oven to 400°F. Spray 6 jumbo muffin cups or 12 regular-size muffin cups with nonstick cooking spray. Stir together muffin mix, oat bran cereal, dark brown sugar, pecans and Goldens & Cherries in a large bowl. Make a well in the center; set aside.

In a 2-cup glass measuring cup, beat eggs slightly. Add milk; whisk to combine. Add enough orange juice to the egg/milk mixture to make 1½ cups of liquid; pour into the dry ingredients and stir just until moistened and combined.

Using a ½-cup measure for jumbo muffins or a ¼-cup measure for regular size muffins, spoon the batter evenly into the muffin cups. Bake jumbo muffins for about 25 minutes or regular muffins for 12-15 minutes, or until muffin tops are golden and a toothpick inserted in the center comes out clean. Cool in pan for 5 minutes. Remove muffins from pans and place on foil to cool a bit longer. Serve warm with butter.

Amelia's Place

In an old factory building constructed in 1924, Amelia's apartment on the third floor is the only existing apartment in downtown Dallas from the 1920's. The six guest rooms are named and decorated in the personal styles of women of all colors who have made profound contributions to Dallas.

Amelia, a feminist from Louisiana who was said to be the best cook in three parishes, offers genuine Southern hospitality.

INNKEEPERS:	Amelia Core Jenkins
ADDRESS:	1775 Young Street
	Dallas, Texas 75201
TELEPHONE:	(214) 651-1775; (888) 651-1775
E-MAIL:	ameliaj@flash.net
WEBSITE:	www.ameliasplace.com
ROOMS:	6 Rooms; Private & shared baths
CHILDREN:	Children age 14 and older welcome
ANIMALS:	Not allowed
HANDICAPPED:	Not handicapped accessible
DIETARY NEEDS:	Will accommodate guests' special dietary needs

Buttermilk Biscuits with Tomato Gravy & Bacon

Makes 5 Servings

Biscuits:
2   cups self-rising flour
1   cup buttermilk (or enough to make a stiff dough)
Vegetable oil (enough to cover bottom of pan generously)

Tomato gravy & bacon:
1   pound bacon
2-3 tablespoons all-purpose flour
1   small onion, finely chopped
1   (14½-ounce) can diced peeled tomatoes
Salt and pepper, to taste

For the biscuits: Preheat oven to 450°F. Put self-rising flour in a bowl. Add enough buttermilk to make a stiff dough. Turn dough out onto a floured surface. With floured hands, knead dough for no longer than 10 seconds. Pinch off 10 biscuit-size pieces of dough and form into round shapes (or roll dough out to ¾-inch thick and cut with a biscuit cutter).

Pour enough oil into an 8-inch round baking pan to generously cover the bottom. Lay each biscuit in the oil, then turn over so both sides are coated. When all biscuits are in the pan, pat biscuits down until sides are touching. Bake for 15 minutes on the top rack of the oven, or until biscuits are golden brown. Serve with tomato gravy or with butter and jelly or molasses.

For the tomato gravy and bacon: Fry bacon in a heavy skillet; drain on paper towels. Pour off grease, reserving 3 tablespoons of bacon grease in the skillet. Add the all-purpose flour; cook, stirring or whisking constantly, until mixture turns a deep chocolate brown. Add the onion; cook over low heat until transparent. Stir in the tomatoes and about 1 cup of water. Season with salt and pepper. Simmer until the gravy reaches the desired consistency. To serve, place hot, split biscuits on plates. Ladle tomato gravy over the biscuits. Serve with the bacon on the side.

Star of Texas

In the evening at the Star of Texas Bed & Breakfast, you may stroll along wooded trails on the inn's 20 acres, or relax under a star-lit sky and be soothed by the sound of the waterfall. Settle down to a blissful night's sleep in a hand-forged iron bed and awaken to singing birds and a wholesome country breakfast served to you in your own cottage.

The Night of Romance package includes a rose bouquet, cheese and crackers, chocolates and a very romantic candlelight meal for two.

INNKEEPERS:	Don & Debbie Morelock
ADDRESS:	650 Morelock Lane
	Brownwood, Texas 76801
TELEPHONE:	(800) 850-2003
E-MAIL:	relaxing@star-of-texas.com
WEBSITE:	www.star-of-texas.com
ROOMS:	1 Suite; 2 Cottages; Private baths
CHILDREN:	Not allowed
ANIMALS:	Call ahead; Resident pets
HANDICAPPED:	Not handicapped accessible
DIETARY NEEDS:	Will accommodate guests' special dietary needs

Cheddar Biscuits

Makes 4 Large Biscuits

"These hearty biscuits are a favorite – there is never a crumb left." – Innkeeper, Star of Texas Bed & Breakfast

1   cup whole-wheat baking mix (such as Hodgson Mill insta-bake mix)
⅓   cup milk
1   tablespoon chopped fresh tarragon (or 1 teaspoon dried)
½   cup (2 ounces) grated cheddar cheese
1½   tablespoons butter, melted
Garlic bread sprinkle (such as McCormick's)

Preheat oven to 425°F. Spray a baking sheet with nonstick cooking spray. In a small bowl, combine baking mix, milk, tarragon and cheese. Form 4 biscuits by dropping dough, about 2 inches apart, onto the baking sheet. Bake for 20 minutes, or until the biscuits are golden brown.

While biscuits are baking, melt butter and garlic sprinkles together. Brush on tops of biscuits just before serving.

George Blucher House

High on the bluff overlooking Corpus Christi Bay, George Anton von Blucher and his bride built their galleried Victorian home in 1904. Now known as the George Blucher House, the inn exudes an understated elegance and the hospitality of days gone by. Nestled quietly beneath towering magnolia, elm, anachua, pecan and oak trees, this historic home sits just across the street from Blucher Park, an internationally renowned bird sanctuary. The inn is just a short stroll to unique downtown shops, upscale restaurants and a sparkling bayfront and marina with colorful sailboats.

INNKEEPERS:	Tracey Love Smith
ADDRESS:	211 North Carrizo
	Corpus Christi, Texas 78401
TELEPHONE:	(361) 884-4884; (866) 884-4884
E-MAIL:	innkeeper@georgeblucherhouse.com
WEBSITE:	www. georgeblucherhouse.com
ROOMS:	5 Rooms; 1 Suite; Private baths
CHILDREN:	Call ahead
ANIMALS:	Not allowed; Resident dog & cat
HANDICAPPED:	Call ahead
DIETARY NEEDS:	Will accommodate guests' special dietary needs

George Blucher House Crunchy Granola

Makes About 9 Cups

"Serve with plain or fruit yogurt, milk or cream. For a real treat, reserve coconut milk (if using fresh coconut slivers in the granola) and pour over the granola instead of the yogurt or milk." ~ Innkeeper, George Blucher House

4	cups old-fashioned rolled oats (not quick-cooking oats)
1	cup wheat germ
½	cup All-Bran Original cereal
2	(6-ounce) packages Planters trail mix (any variety without candy)
2-3	tablespoons sesame seeds
1	cup honey
1	cup canola oil
1	teaspoon cinnamon
1	(6-ounce) package dried Mariani Berries 'N Cherries (a blend of dried blueberries, strawberries, cherries and cranberries)

10-12 dried apricots, chopped
Fresh or dried coconut slivers (optional)

Preheat oven to 300°F. In a large bowl, combine oats, wheat germ, All-Bran, trail mix and sesame seeds; set aside. In a small saucepan, heat together honey, oil and cinnamon; stir until well mixed. Pour hot honey mixture over oat mixture; stir to combine. Spread evenly onto 2 large, greased baking sheets. Bake for 30-40 minutes, stirring every 10 minutes, until the mixture is toasted a light golden brown. Cool completely, stirring occasionally to keep the granola from "clumping."

When granola is cool, add Berries 'n Cherries, apricots and coconut; mix well. Store airtight in the refrigerator or freezer (if frozen, allow to come to room temperature before serving). This granola will keep for months.

Brook House

The Brook House was built in 1922. It has been lovingly restored to its present-day country charm. High ceilings, original windows and antique-filled rooms create a relaxed atmosphere and a comfortable retreat from your busy world.

A full breakfast is served in the beautiful dining room near a warm fireplace or, weather permitting, on the veranda.

INNKEEPERS:	Matt & Lisa Wiedemann
ADDRESS:	609 West 33rd
	Austin, Texas 78705
TELEPHONE:	(512) 459-0534; (800) 871-8908
E-MAIL:	brookhouse@earthlink.net
WEBSITE:	www.austinbedandbreakfast.com
ROOMS:	6 Rooms; 1 Suite; 1 Cottage; Private baths
CHILDREN:	Welcome
ANIMALS:	Welcome in certain rooms
HANDICAPPED:	Call ahead
DIETARY NEEDS:	Will accommodate guests' special dietary needs

Brook House Granola

Makes 10 Cups

6	cups old-fashioned rolled oats (not quick-cooking oats)
1	cup wheat germ
1	cup All-Bran Original cereal
1	cup chopped nuts
1	cup shredded coconut
½	cup packed brown sugar
1	teaspoon cinnamon
1	cup honey
½	cup canola oil

Combine oats, wheat germ, cereal, nuts and coconut in a very large bowl. Add brown sugar and cinnamon; mix well. Combine honey and oil in a microwavable bowl. Heat in the microwave for about 45 seconds, then stir well. Pour honey mixture over oat mixture; mix thoroughly.

Preheat oven to 300°F. Spread granola mixture evenly onto a large, rimmed baking sheet (line the baking sheet with parchment paper, if desired). Bake for 25-30 minutes, stirring every 5-10 minutes, allowing the granola to brown evenly. (If you do not line the baking sheet with parchment paper, stir the granola occasionally as it cools to keep it from sticking to the pan.) Cool the granola completely and store it in an airtight container. This granola freezes well.

Coffee Cakes, Rolls & Scones

Coffee Cakes, Rolls & Scones

A Beckmann Inn

The wonderful wrap-around porch at A Beckmann Inn & Carriage House warmly welcomes guests through the rare burl pine door to the main house. The inn allows guests to experience Victorian hospitality in a quiet and tranquil atmosphere.

The wicker furniture on the sun porch invites guests to relax and enjoy the "welcome tea" which includes complimentary chocolates and butter cookies.

INNKEEPERS:	Betty Jo & Don Schwartz
ADDRESS:	222 East Guenther Street
	San Antonio, Texas 78204
TELEPHONE:	(210) 229-1449; (800) 945-1449
E-MAIL:	beckinn@swbell.net
WEBSITE:	www.beckmanninn.com
ROOMS:	5 Rooms; Private baths
CHILDREN:	Children age 12 and older welcome
ANIMALS:	Not allowed
HANDICAPPED:	Not handicapped accessible
DIETARY NEEDS:	Will accommodate guests' special dietary needs

Rhubarb Crumb Coffee Cake

Makes 12 Servings

Batter:
2   cups flour
1½   cups sugar
2   tablespoons baking powder
1½   sticks (¾ cup) butter, melted
2   eggs
1   cup milk

Rhubarb mixture:
2   cups sliced fresh rhubarb
1   cup sugar
3   tablespoons flour

Crumb topping:
2   tablespoons flour
2   tablespoons sugar
2   tablespoons butter, chilled

For the batter: Preheat oven to 350°F. Spray a 9x13-inch baking pan with nonstick cooking spray. Mix flour, sugar, baking powder and melted butter in a medium bowl. Add eggs and milk; stir until combined. Pour batter into the pan.

For the rhubarb mixture: Combine rhubarb, sugar and flour in a bowl; spoon evenly over the batter in the pan.

For the crumb topping: Combine flour, sugar and butter in a small bowl. Using a fork or your fingers, mix until crumbly; sprinkle over the rhubarb.

Bake for 45-55 minutes, or until a toothpick inserted in the center comes out clean. Cool on a wire rack.

A Long Stay

A Long Stay is reminiscent of an old south Texas ranch with the innkeepers' personal touches intermingled throughout the home. The stables and barn retain their original look, but these buildings have been converted to very comfortable and unique accommodations.

A Long Stay was established in 1998 with a vision of providing a calm and peaceful place for contemplative thought, renewal and celebration.

INNKEEPERS:	Pat Long & Linda Long
ADDRESS:	137 Old San Antonio Road
	Boerne, Texas 78006
TELEPHONE:	(830) 249-1234; (877) 566-4782
E-MAIL:	longstay@gvtc.com
WEBSITE:	www.alongstay.com
ROOMS:	4 Rooms; 2 Suites; 1 Cottage; Private baths
CHILDREN:	Welcome
ANIMALS:	Small dogs allowed; Resident dog, goats & horse
HANDICAPPED:	Not handicapped accessible
DIETARY NEEDS:	Will accommodate guests' special dietary needs

Sausage Blueberry Coffee Cake

Makes 12 Servings

1	pound Jimmy Dean low-fat sausage
1	stick (½ cup) butter, room temperature
¾	cup white sugar
¼	cup packed brown sugar
2	cups flour
1	teaspoon baking powder
½	teaspoon baking soda
2	eggs
1	(8-ounce) carton sour cream
1	cup blueberries
¾	cup chopped pecans

Glaze:

½	cup sugar
2	tablespoons cornstarch
½	cup water
2	cups blueberries
½	teaspoon lemon juice

Chopped pecans, as many or as few as desired

Preheat oven to 350°F. Spray a 9x13-inch baking pan with nonstick cooking spray. Brown the sausage thoroughly; drain and cool. Beat butter, white sugar and brown sugar in a large bowl. Sift together flour, baking powder and baking soda; add to butter mixture. Add eggs, one at a time, beating well after each addition. Stir in sour cream. Gently fold in blueberries and pecans.

Spread cooked sausage into the pan. Spread batter evenly over the sausage. (The cake can be prepared up to this point the night before and refrigerated. The next morning, let it come to room temperature before baking.) Bake for 35-40 minutes. While the cake is baking, make the glaze.

For the glaze: Combine sugar, cornstarch and water in a saucepan over medium heat. Bring to a boil, lower heat and simmer until thickened, about 5 minutes. Add blueberries and lemon juice; cook for 5 minutes more. Pour glaze over cake. Sprinkle with pecans. Serve warm.

Rosevine Inn

The Rosevine Inn Bed & Breakfast is conveniently located in Tyler, with numerous antique and craft shops only a short distance away. Visitors can explore Dewberry Plantation, East Texas Symphony Orchestra Association, Tiger Creek Wildlife Refuge and the Tyler Rose Museum.

The Lodge Room is modeled after a room in a museum in Strasbourg, France. It is intimate and refined, yet rustic and quaint. A queen-size bed is nestled into one alcove, while a six-foot soaking tub is tucked into another.

INNKEEPERS:	Rebecca & Bert Powell
ADDRESS:	415 South Vine
	Tyler, Texas 75702
TELEPHONE:	(903) 592-2221
EMAIL:	rosevine@iamerica.net
WEBSITE:	www.rosevine.com
ROOMS:	6 Rooms; 1 Suite; 2 Cottages; Private baths
CHILDREN:	Children age 5 and older welcome
ANIMALS:	Not allowed; Resident outdoor cats
HANDICAPPED:	Not handicapped accessible
DIETARY NEEDS:	Will accommodate guests' special dietary needs

Fresh Apple Coffee Cake

Serves 10 to 12

"Thelma, a lady who worked for my grandmother for years, gave me this recipe. I think of both of them every time I make it." ~ Innkeeper, Rosevine Inn B&B

3	cups flour
1½	teaspoons baking soda
½	teaspoon nutmeg
½	teaspoon cinnamon
½	teaspoon salt
2	cups sugar
1½	cups vegetable oil
2	eggs
3	cups peeled and chopped Granny Smith apples
1	cup chopped pecans
1½	cups sifted powdered sugar
1	tablespoon butter, melted
1	tablespoon lemon juice

Water (about 3-4 teaspoons)

Preheat oven to 350°F. Spray a 9- or 10-inch springform pan or a 12-cup Bundt pan with nonstick cooking spray. Sift together flour, baking soda, nutmeg, cinnamon and salt in a large bowl. Make a well in the center of the dry ingredients; set aside. In a medium bowl, combine sugar, oil and eggs; add to the dry ingredients, stirring to combine (the batter will be thick). Stir in apples and pecans. Spoon batter into baking pan.

Bake for 60 minutes, or until a toothpick inserted in the center comes out clean. Cool cake in pan for 20 minutes. If using a springform pan, remove the sides of the pan after 20 minutes. If using a Bundt pan, remove the cake from the pan after 20 minutes. Finish cooling the cake on a wire rack.

While cake is cooling, make a lemon glaze by combining powdered sugar, melted butter and lemon juice in a small bowl. Stir in enough water to reach a drizzling consistency. When cake has completely cooled, drizzle with the lemon glaze.

The Lodges at Lost Maples

All of the cabins at The Lodges at Lost Maples have hardwood flooring, spacious cathedral ceilings and a quaint living room. Whether you've spent the day hiking at Lost Maples State Natural Area, tubing the Frio or horseback riding in the hills, you'll be glad to kick back in a hammock and enjoy the hill country sunset. Each morning, you will awaken to freshly baked breakfast treats such as apricot-white chocolate scones, pecan twists or The Lodge's special rustic chocolate, warm-center chocolate muffins.

INNKEEPERS:	The Hathorn Family
ADDRESS:	77 Lower Sabinal River Road
	Vanderpool, Texas 78885
TELEPHONE:	(830) 966-5178; (877) 216-5627
E-MAIL:	lodges@lostmaplescabins.com
WEBSITE:	www.lostmaplescabins.com
ROOMS:	5 Cabins; Private baths
CHILDREN:	Welcome
ANIMALS:	Not allowed
HANDICAPPED:	Not handicapped accessible
DIETARY NEEDS:	Will accommodate guests' special dietary needs

Almost Sinful Cinnamon Rolls

Makes 12 Rolls

"Something this easy shouldn't be this good!" ~ Innkeeper, The Lodges at Lost Maples

Dough:
2	cups flour
2	tablespoons sugar
4	teaspoons baking powder
1	teaspoon salt
½	stick (¼ cup) butter, chilled
1	cup milk, chilled

Filling:
⅓	cup butter, softened
1	cup packed brown sugar
3	teaspoons cinnamon

Glaze:
½ cup powdered sugar
Milk (about 2-3 teaspoons)

For the dough: Preheat oven to 400°F. Spray 12 muffin cups with nonstick cooking spray. Combine flour, sugar, baking powder and salt in a large bowl. Cut in butter until crumbly. Make a well in the center. Add the milk and stir to form a soft dough. Turn out onto a floured surface. Knead 8-10 times. Roll dough into a ⅓-inch thick, 10x12-inch rectangle.

For the filling: Combine softened butter, brown sugar and cinnamon; sprinkle onto dough. Roll up, jelly-roll style, starting from the long side. Seal the seam. Slice the roll into 12 pieces. Put pieces, cut-sides-down, into the muffin cups. Bake for 20-22 minutes. Remove from oven. Cool for 1 minute, then turn out onto a wire rack. Cool slightly, then drizzle with glaze. Serve warm or cold.

For the glaze: Put powdered sugar in a small bowl. Stir in enough milk to reach a drizzling consistency.

A Yellow Rose

Prepare to be pampered during your stay at A Yellow Rose Bed & Breakfast. This beautiful 130-year-old Victorian is located in the King William Historic District in downtown San Antonio. Relax in spacious guest rooms with luxurious amenities such as Godiva Chocolates and Caswell Massey bath products.

After breakfast, enjoy a day of strolling on the River Walk, do a little shopping or take in an exhibit at one of the many museums in the area.

INNKEEPERS:	Deb & Kit Walker
ADDRESS:	229 Madison
	San Antonio, Texas 78204
TELEPHONE:	(210) 229-9903; (800) 950-9903
E-MAIL:	info@ayellowrose.com
WEBSITE:	www.ayellowrose.com
ROOMS:	5 Rooms; 1 Suite; Private baths
CHILDREN:	Children age 12 and older welcome
ANIMALS:	Not allowed
HANDICAPPED:	Not handicapped accessible
DIETARY NEEDS:	Will accommodate guests' special dietary needs

Sausage Puffs

Makes 4 Servings

You can also create your own delicious stuffings for these puffs. Try scrambled eggs with cooked crumbled bacon or a mixture of chopped artichoke hearts and cream cheese.

1	can croissant dough, unbaked
8	ounces breakfast sausage
5	tablespoons cream cheese
1	egg white
2	tablespoons sesame seeds

Preheat oven to 350°F. Cook sausage in a medium skillet until cooked through; drain any grease. Add cream cheese while the sausage is still warm; stir until completely combined.

Spread ½ of the croissant pieces on a greased baking sheet. Spoon sausage mixture over the croissant. Cover with the remaining croissant pieces; crimp the dough edges together to seal. With a pastry brush, lightly brush egg white over the top of the dough. Sprinkle with sesame seeds. Bake for 12-15 minutes. Serve warm.

Gruene Mansion Inn

After settling in to your room at the Gruene Mansion Inn, you can dance in Gruene Hall, float the Guadalupe, shop downtown Gruene for "serious antiques," clothes, handmade furniture and pottery, Texas gifts and home furnishings, or just soak up the soul of Texas without moving your car.

Arrington's B&B Journal listed the Gruene Mansion Inn as one of the "Top 15 Most Romantic Bed & Breakfasts in America."

INNKEEPERS:	Cecil & Judi Eager
ADDRESS:	1275 Gruene Road
	New Braunfels, Texas 78130
TELEPHONE:	(830) 629-2641
E-MAIL:	frontdesk@gruenemansioninn.com
WEBSITE:	www.gruenemansioninn.com
ROOMS:	30 Rooms; 12 Suites; 1 Cottage; Private baths
CHILDREN:	Welcome
ANIMALS:	Not allowed
HANDICAPPED:	Handicapped accessible
DIETARY NEEDS:	Will accommodate guests' special dietary needs

Gruene Mansion Blintzes

Makes 8 Scones

"We have a line at the kitchen door for this recipe! The 'blintzes' can also be frozen for later use." - Innkeeper, Gruene Mansion Inn

1   loaf sliced white bread, crusts removed
1   (8-ounce) package cream cheese, room temperature
¼   cup powdered sugar
4-5 tablespoons butter, melted
Cinnamon/sugar (½ cup sugar mixed with 1 tablespoon cinnamon)

Preheat oven to 350°F. Spray a baking sheet with nonstick cooking spray. Roll out crustless bread slices with a rolling pin into ¼-inch thick rectangles. Mix cream cheese and powdered sugar in a small bowl until smooth. Spread cream cheese mixture on one side of bread rectangles.

Roll up bread rectangles, jelly-roll style, starting with the short side. Brush outside of each blintz with melted butter. Roll in cinnamon/sugar until well covered. Put blintzes in freezer for 10 minutes. Cut blintzes in half and place on baking sheet. Bake for 15-20 minutes. Serve hot.

The Carleton House

Located in the heart of historic downtown Bonham, just one hour northeast of Dallas, is the historic Carleton House Bed & Breakfast. The house was built in 1888 by A.J. Clendenen, who operated a grocery on the square. In 1914, Dr. J.C. Carleton purchased the home for his family and had the house wired for electricity.

Lillian's Room overlooks the gardens and features a king-size bed, antiques, quilts and lacy touches for the romantics.

INNKEEPERS:	Karen & Steve Halbrook
ADDRESS:	803 North Main
	Bonham, Texas 75418
TELEPHONE:	(903) 583-2779; (800) 382-8033
E-MAIL:	information@carletonhouse.com
WEBSITE:	www.carletonhouse.com
ROOMS:	5 Rooms; 1 Suite; Private baths
CHILDREN:	Welcome
ANIMALS:	Call ahead
HANDICAPPED:	Handicapped accessible
DIETARY NEEDS:	Will accommodate guests' special dietary needs

Apricot Cinnamon Scones

Makes 10 Small Scones

1½	cups flour
1½	teaspoons baking powder
⅛	teaspoon baking soda
½	teaspoon salt
1	tablespoon sugar
3	tablespoons shortening
1	egg
¾	cup buttermilk
¼	cup chopped dried apricots
¼	cup cinnamon chips
2	tablespoons butter, melted
½	cup powdered sugar
½	teaspoon vanilla extract

Dash of cinnamon (optional)
1-2 teaspoons water or milk

Preheat oven to 400°F. Lightly spray an 8-inch pie pan or round baking pan with nonstick cooking spray. Sift flour, baking powder, baking soda, salt and sugar into a large bowl. Cut in shortening with a pastry cutter until mixture resembles coarse crumbs; make a well in the center. In a small bowl, whisk egg until light in color. Add buttermilk. Mix well, then add all at once to the dry ingredients. Using a fork, stir just until moistened (dough will be sticky). Let stand for 5 minutes. Gently stir in apricots and cinnamon chips.

Spoon about ¼ cup of dough onto a floured surface; lightly dust with flour. With floured hands, shape into an elongated wedge. Shake off excess flour. Place wedge into pan with the point toward the center. Repeat until all the dough is used and you have created a circle of scones (they will be touching). Brush tops of scones with melted butter. Bake for 15-20 minutes, or until golden brown. Remove from pan and let cool for 10 minutes on a wire rack.

Combine powdered sugar, vanilla, cinnamon and enough water or milk to reach a drizzling consistency. Stir until smooth, then drizzle on cooled scones. Serve warm with jam or jelly.

Brown Pelican Inn

The Brown Pelican Inn offers some of the finest accommodations in south Texas. Situated on the quiet bay shoreline of the famed South Padre Island, the inn boasts eight elegant guest rooms appointed with American and English antiques, each with a private bath.

Several rooms have spectacular bay views, and the covered porch is a favorite vantage point from which to enjoy the sunset.

INNKEEPERS:	Chris & Yves de Diesbach
ADDRESS:	207 West Aries
	South Padre Island, Texas 78597
TELEPHONE:	(956) 761-2722
E-MAIL:	innkeeper@brownpelican.com
WEBSITE:	www.brownpelican.com
ROOMS:	8 Rooms; Private baths
CHILDREN:	Children age 12 and older welcome
ANIMALS:	Not allowed
HANDICAPPED:	Handicapped accessible
DIETARY NEEDS:	Will accommodate guests' special dietary needs

Brown Pelican Scones

Makes 12 to 14 Scones

Great for afternoon tea! These scones are best served warm from the oven with crème fraîche and strawberry preserves.

3   cups unbleached all-purpose flour
1   cup whole-wheat bread flour
5½   teaspoons baking powder
½   cup sugar
1   stick (½ cup) butter, chilled and cut into pieces
1   egg
1   cup buttermilk

Preheat oven to 400°F. Sift together all-purpose flour, whole-wheat flour, baking powder and sugar into a large bowl. Add butter pieces; mix with your fingers until crumbly. Whisk together egg and buttermilk in a small bowl; add to the dry ingredients and stir just until combined.

Put dough on a lightly floured surface and knead lightly. Roll out dough to a ¾-inch thickness. Cut dough with a biscuit cutter. Place scones about 1½-inches apart on an ungreased baking sheet. Bake for 10-12 minutes, or until lightly browned. Serve warm.

A Yellow Rose

S taying at A Yellow Rose Bed & Breakfast is as comfortable as staying with good friends – except the innkeepers place Godiva chocolates on your pillow and serve a wonderful breakfast in your room. Innkeepers Deb and Kit Walker strive to provide guests with the same quality and comforts that they appreciate when they are traveling.

"The wonderful breakfast just added to the beauty and perfection of a night I will remember forever." ~ Guest, A Yellow Rose Bed & Breakfast

INNKEEPERS:	Deb & Kit Walker
ADDRESS:	229 Madison
	San Antonio, Texas 78204
TELEPHONE:	(210) 229-9903; (800) 950-9903
E-MAIL:	info@ayellowrose.com
WEBSITE:	www.ayellowrose.com
ROOMS:	5 Rooms; 1 Suite; Private baths
CHILDREN:	Children age 12 and older welcome
ANIMALS:	Not allowed
HANDICAPPED:	Not handicapped accessible
DIETARY NEEDS:	Will accommodate guests' special dietary needs

Buttermilk Scone for Two

Makes 2 Servings

Plan ahead – this large scone takes 30 minutes to bake.

1   cup flour
1½   tablespoons sugar
1   teaspoon baking powder
⅛   teaspoon baking soda
½   stick (¼ cup) butter, chilled and cut into small pieces
3   tablespoons currants
¼   teaspoon grated orange zest
¼   cup buttermilk, more if needed
Cinnamon-sugar (⅛ teaspoon cinnamon mixed with ½ teaspoon sugar)
Butter and jam, for serving

Preheat oven to 375°F. Sift together flour, sugar, baking powder and baking soda in a medium bowl. Add butter pieces to dry ingredients; rub with your fingers to form fine crumbs. Stir in currants and orange zest. Make a well in the center of the flour mixture; pour in the buttermilk and stir with a fork until dough holds together (add up to 2 more tablespoons of buttermilk, if needed for dough to hold together).

Pat dough into a ball and knead on a lightly floured surface, about 5-6 times. Shape dough into a smooth ball and place into a greased 8- or 9-inch round cake or pie pan. Sprinkle with cinnamon-sugar.

Bake for 10 minutes. Remove from oven and, with a sharp knife, quickly cut a cross-shape, ½-inch deep, across the top of the scone. Return the scone to the oven and bake for about 20 minutes more, or until golden brown. Serve warm with butter and jam.

Green Gables

C ome enjoy the amenities of this bed and breakfast hideaway on the Little Blanco River in the beautiful Texas Hill Country. Located on a secluded, private 14-acre estate, Green Gables Bed & Breakfast provides an escape from city noise, ringing telephones and the bustle of everyday life.

Relax beneath the centuries-old pecan and cypress trees that nestle along the banks of the crystal-clear, spring-fed waters of the Little Blanco.

INNKEEPERS:	Glen & Sue McFarlin
ADDRESS:	401 Green Gables
	Blanco, Texas 78606
TELEPHONE:	(830) 833-5931; (888) 833-5931
E-MAIL:	mcfarlin@moment.net
WEBSITE:	www.greengables-tx.com
ROOMS:	1 Suite; 2 Cottages; Private baths
CHILDREN:	Welcome
ANIMALS:	Not allowed; Resident dogs & cats
HANDICAPPED:	Not handicapped accessible
DIETARY NEEDS:	Will accommodate guests' special dietary needs

Aunt Dora's Apricot Currant Scones

Makes 8 Scones

"Fresh breads made from scratch are a mainstay of our breakfasts. These scones are a favorite with our guests." - Innkeeper, Green Gables Bed & Breakfast

2	cups flour
3	tablespoons sugar
½	teaspoon salt
1	tablespoon baking powder
1	stick (½ cup) butter, chilled and cut into small pieces
¼	cup currants
¼	cup chopped apricots
⅔	cup milk
1	egg, beaten

Butter, for serving
Jam, for serving

Preheat oven to 400°F. Lightly butter a baking sheet (if not nonstick). Combine flour, sugar, salt and baking powder in a medium bowl. Add butter; mix with your fingers to combine and form a soft crumble. Stir in currants and apricots. Add milk; stir just until a soft dough is formed.

Turn dough out onto a floured surface. With lightly floured hands, knead a couple of times to form a loose ball; pat out on the baking sheet into an 8-inch circle. Using a floured, serrated knife, cut the dough into 8 wedges. Wiggle the knife back and forth to separate the edges so that air can circulate between the scones. Brush the tops of the scones with beaten egg.

Bake for 18-20 minutes, or until golden brown and cooked through. Cool on a wire rack for about 5 minutes. Serve warm with butter and jam.

Pancakes & Waffles

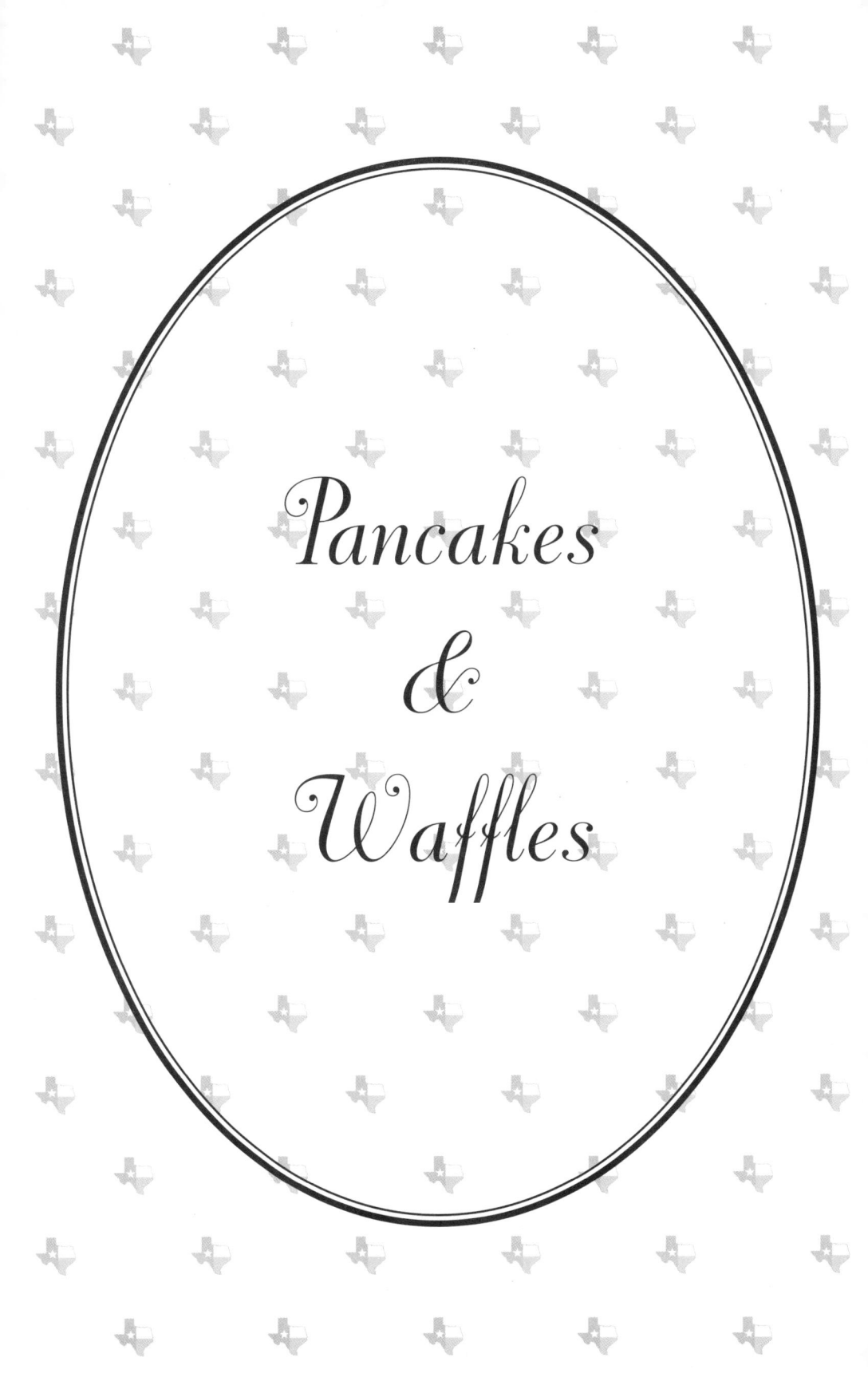

Pancakes

&

Waffles

Star of Texas

The landscape at the Star of Texas Bed & Breakfast is a certified Texas Wildscape. There is a nature trail that winds through the inn's 20 acres. You will be delighted by deer, turkey, squirrel and many varieties of birds. Along the trail, you will find little treasures of art and fun objects to mark your way.

Enjoy the prayer garden, or sit on the bench overlooking the meadow and watch for Red Tail hawks.

INNKEEPERS:	Don & Debbie Morelock
ADDRESS:	650 Morelock Lane
	Brownwood, Texas 76801
TELEPHONE:	(800) 850-2003
E-MAIL:	relaxing@star-of-texas.com
WEBSITE:	www.star-of-texas.com
ROOMS:	1 Suite; 2 Cottages; Private baths
CHILDREN:	Not allowed
ANIMALS:	Call ahead; Resident pets
HANDICAPPED:	Not handicapped accessible
DIETARY NEEDS:	Will accommodate guests' special dietary needs

Fall Pancakes with Apple Spice Syrup

Makes 4 Servings

"These pancakes are great for crisp fall mornings. Top with fresh whipped cream and serve with bacon." ~ Innkeeper, Star of Texas Bed & Breakfast

2	cups whole-wheat baking mix (such as Hodgson Mill insta-bake mix)
½	teaspoon cinnamon
2	eggs
1¼	cups milk
½	cup applesauce
1	teaspoon vanilla extract

Whipped cream and chopped pecans, for garnish
Apple spice syrup (recipe follows)

Combine baking mix and cinnamon in a medium bowl. In another bowl, combine eggs, milk, applesauce and vanilla; add to dry ingredients and stir until combined. Preheat a greased griddle or skillet over medium heat. Spoon batter by ¼-cupfuls onto griddle. Cook until pancakes are golden on both sides. Serve pancakes topped with whipped cream and sprinkled with pecans. Offer warm apple spice syrup on the side.

Apple spice syrup:

¼	cup brown sugar
2	tablespoons cornstarch
¼	teaspoon cinnamon
⅛	teaspoon nutmeg
1½	cups apple juice

Combine brown sugar, cornstarch, cinnamon and nutmeg in a medium saucepan. Gradually stir in apple juice until smooth. Stirring constantly, bring to a boil over medium heat. Boil for 1 minute, until the mixture thickens. Remove from heat. Serve warm. (The syrup can be prepared ahead, covered and refrigerated. Gently reheat syrup in the microwave or on the stove when ready to use.)

Brackenridge House

Brackenridge House innkeeper Bennie Blansett is a retired Air Force Colonel. His wife, Sue, left her job as a university administrator when they launched their second career as innkeepers. They are native Texans who chose to retire in San Antonio after living all over the United States and in Guam, the Philippines and Germany.

The Blansetts can tell you stories of the way San Antonio used to be. Both are well versed on places to go in San Antonio and the Texas Hill Country.

INNKEEPERS:	Bennie & Sue Blansett
ADDRESS:	230 Madison
	San Antonio, Texas 78204
TELEPHONE:	(210) 271-3442; (800) 221-1412
E-MAIL:	benniesueb@aol.com
WEBSITE:	www.brackenridgehouse.com
ROOMS:	2 Rooms; 3 Suites; 1 Cottage; Private baths
CHILDREN:	Welcome in cottage; Age 12 and older in main house
ANIMALS:	Allowed in cottage
HANDICAPPED:	Not handicapped accessible
DIETARY NEEDS:	Will accommodate guests' special dietary needs

French Baked Pancake

Makes 8 Large Servings

Beautiful presentation! Great taste!

1   stick (½ cup) butter, room temperature, plus 3 tablespoons butter, melted
4   tablespoons sugar
3   eggs plus 2 eggs
2   cups flour
1½ teaspoons baking powder
1¼ cups milk
3   cups small curd cottage cheese
1   teaspoon salt
1   (21-ounce) can blueberry pie filling
¾   cup blueberry syrup (about ½ of a 12-ounce bottle)
1   cup sour cream
1   teaspoon vanilla extract
2   tablespoons powdered sugar
Grated zest of 1 orange, for garnish

Preheat oven to 350°F. Spray a 9x13-inch baking pan with nonstick cooking spray. Combine the 1 stick of butter and sugar in a large bowl. Add 3 eggs; beat well. Combine flour and baking powder. Mix flour mixture and milk alternately into butter mixture. Pour ½ of batter in pan.

Mix cottage cheese, 2 eggs, the 3 tablespoons melted butter and salt in a medium bowl. Spread over the batter in the pan. Top with remaining batter. Bake for 60 minutes, or until golden brown.

Mix and heat blueberry pie filling and syrup together in a saucepan to make a blueberry sauce. Mix sour cream, vanilla and powdered sugar together in a small bowl to make a sour cream sauce.

Cut baked pancake into squares. Serve with blueberry sauce and a dollop of sour cream sauce. Sprinkle with orange zest.

The Inn of Many Faces

S et on two acres of towering pine trees, the Inn of Many Faces was built in 1897 by J.B. McDougall, one of Denison's founding fathers. Recently restored, the house is now a comfortable retreat lovingly managed by Charlie and Gloria Morton.

Surprises await you at every turn. Whether enjoying the garden or soaking in the whirlpool tub, the inn's collection of whimsical faces greet you – hence the name "The Inn of Many Faces."

INNKEEPERS:	Charlie & Gloria Morton
ADDRESS:	412 West Morton Street
	Denison, Texas 75020
TELEPHONE:	(903) 465-4639
E-MAIL:	theinn@texoma.net
WEBSITE:	www.theinnofmanyfaces.com
ROOMS:	4 Rooms; Private baths
CHILDREN:	Children age 11 and older welcome
ANIMALS:	Not allowed
HANDICAPPED:	Not handicapped accessible
DIETARY NEEDS:	Will accommodate guests' special dietary needs

Baked German Apple Pancake

Makes 5 Servings

"A favorite dish of our guests!" - Innkeeper, Inn of Many Faces

Apple mixture:
3   large Granny Smith apples, peeled, cored and sliced
2   tablespoons butter
½   cup white sugar
½   cup brown sugar
2   teaspoons ground cinnamon
¼   teaspoon salt

Pancake batter:
6   eggs, beaten
1   cup milk
1   cup flour
2   teaspoons white sugar
¼   teaspoon salt
3   tablespoons butter, melted

For the apple mixture: Preheat oven to 450°F. Spray five 5-inch diameter ramekins (the ramekins should each have a 1½-cup capacity) with nonstick cooking spray. Melt butter in a skillet over medium-low heat. Stir in the butter, white sugar, brown sugar, cinnamon and salt. Add the apple and cook until slightly soft (avoid letting the mixture boil to keep the sugar from crystallizing). Divide the apples equally among the ramekins.

For the pancake batter: Mix all of the pancake batter ingredients in a large bowl, stirring just until combined (the batter will be lumpy). Pour over the top of the apple mixture in each ramekin.

Bake for 18 minutes. Lower oven temperature to 350°F and bake for 7-10 more minutes. Serve. (You do not need additional syrup for serving as the apple mixture makes its own syrup during baking.)

Vieh's

E xperience the friendly hospitality of south Texas in this comfortable ranch-style home on 15 acres, just three miles from Old Mexico, and centrally located between Brownsville, Santa Ana and Laguna Atascosa. A 10 acre pond across the back of the property offers a relaxed walking area and the opportunity to view a variety of area wildlife.

There are two butterfly gardens on the property at Vieh's where you can see such beauties as Pixies, Giant Swallowtails and Admirals.

INNKEEPERS:	Lana & Charles Vieh
ADDRESS:	18413 Landrum Park Road
	San Benito, Texas 78586
TELEPHONE:	(956) 425-4651
E-MAIL:	viehbb@aol.com
WEBSITE:	www.vieh.com
ROOMS:	4 Rooms; 1 Cottage; Private & shared baths
CHILDREN:	Welcome
ANIMALS:	Welcome; Call ahead; Resident parrots & horses
HANDICAPPED:	Handicapped accessible
DIETARY NEEDS:	Will accommodate guests' special dietary needs

Lana's Cornmeal Pancakes

Makes 4 Servings (12 Pancakes)

1	cup whole-wheat flour
1	cup yellow cornmeal
1	tablespoon baking powder
1	teaspoon baking soda
1	tablespoon sugar
1½	cups buttermilk
¼	cup cooking oil
1	egg, separated

Syrup, for serving

Sift together whole-wheat flour, cornmeal, baking powder, baking soda and sugar into a large bowl. Combine buttermilk, oil and egg yolk in a medium bowl; add to the dry ingredients and mix just until moistened. In another bowl, beat egg white until stiff, then gently fold into batter (small bits of egg white will still be visible). (If a thinner batter is desired, add up to ½ cup more buttermilk.)

Preheat a lightly greased griddle or skillet over medium heat. Spoon batter onto griddle. Cook until pancakes are golden on both sides. The pancakes are done when golden. Serve with syrup.

Historic Moses Hughes Ranch

1856

Guests of the Historic Moses Hughes Ranch can hike, play in the creek, lounge by the springs or on the upstairs wooden porch, or snuggle by the fireplaces. There is shopping and dining in historic Lampasas, Wild Cave tours (walking and crawling), eagle watching (in season), golf, fishing, museums, historic sites, fabulous lakes, vineyards and festivals.

The Courtyard Casita Suite is furnished in Spanish colonial antiques and has floor-to-ceiling windows facing the beautiful and tranquil courtyard.

INNKEEPERS:	Al & Beverly Solomon
ADDRESS:	7075 West FM 580
	Lampasas, Texas 76550
TELEPHONE:	(512) 556-5923
E-MAIL:	mhrbb@n-link.com
WEBSITE:	www.moseshughesranch.com
ROOMS:	3 Rooms; Private baths
CHILDREN:	Children age 15 and older welcome
ANIMALS:	Not allowed; Resident outdoor cats
HANDICAPPED:	Not handicapped accessible
DIETARY NEEDS:	Will accommodate guests' special dietary needs

Al's Apple Thyme Puff Daddy

Makes 6 Servings

"Al likes to make this recipe in the fall, when all the beautiful apples arrive at the market. The aroma alone brings eager guests to the table." – Innkeeper, Historic Moses Hughes Ranch Bed & Breakfast

3   eggs
¾   cup flour
¾   cup milk
2   tart green apples (such as Granny Smith), very thinly sliced
1-2   teaspoons lemon juice
¼   cup packed brown sugar
2   tablespoons chopped fresh thyme
Maple syrup, for serving

Preheat oven to 425°F. Spray a 9-inch glass pie pan with nonstick cooking spray. Combine eggs, flour and milk in a medium bowl until just blended (the batter will be lumpy). Pour batter into pie pan.

Toss apple slices with lemon juice in a medium bowl. Add brown sugar and thyme; toss again. Arrange apple slices on top of the batter in a circular pattern, overlapping the slices to fit.

Bake for 20-25 minutes, or until puffed and golden brown. Cut into wedges and serve with maple syrup, if desired.

Roadrunner Farm

R oadrunner Farm Bed & Breakfast is located in a Texas Limestone house that was featured in *Southern Living* magazine. The inn is located on 32 secluded, gently rolling acres of horse country, close to the Dallas/Ft. Worth area and minutes from Denton.

Accommodations include two spacious bedrooms with private baths. Other amenities include a beautiful swimming pool, wood-burning fireplaces, wooded nature trails.

INNKEEPERS:	Jan Farris Michie
ADDRESS:	10501 Fincher Road
	Argyle, Texas 76226
TELEPHONE:	(940) 241-3089
E-MAIL:	jan-michie@roadrunnerfarm.com
WEBSITE:	www.roadrunnerfarm.com
ROOMS:	2 Rooms; Private baths
CHILDREN:	Children age 10 and older welcome
ANIMALS:	Not allowed; Resident dog
HANDICAPPED:	Not handicapped accessible
DIETARY NEEDS:	Will accommodate guests' special dietary needs

Maple Bacon Cheddar Cake

Makes 8 Servings

A unique and tasty baked pancake. "This recipe is a hit with young people, as well as adults." ~ Innkeeper, Roadrunner Farm Bed & Breakfast

18   slices uncooked bacon (about 1 pound), cut into ½-inch pieces
1½   cups baking mix (such as Bisquick)
1   tablespoon sugar
2   eggs
¾   cup milk
¼   cup real maple syrup, plus additional for serving
Dash of nutmeg
2   cups (8 ounces) grated cheddar cheese, divided
2   tablespoons butter, melted
Fresh fruit, for garnish

Preheat oven to 425°F. Spray a 9x13-inch baking dish with nonstick cooking spray. In a large skillet, fry bacon pieces until crisp; drain and keep warm. Combine baking mix, sugar, eggs, milk, ¼ cup maple syrup and nutmeg in a large bowl; beat well until smooth. Stir in 1 cup of grated cheese. Pour the batter into the baking dish.

Bake for 12-15 minutes, or until the top of the pancake is a light golden brown and springs back when lightly touched. Remove from oven. While hot, brush the top with melted butter. Sprinkle with the remaining 1 cup of cheese. Top with bacon pieces. Cut into serving pieces. Serve with maple syrup and garnish with colorful fresh fruit.

Note: The bacon can be prepared in advance. If desired, it can be cooked whole and then crumbled (you'll need about 1½ cups of crumbled bacon). You can also use purchased precooked bacon. Briefly heat the cooked bacon in the microwave before topping the pancake.

The Cotton Palace

The Cotton Palace Bed & Breakfast lavishes guests with fine furnishings in comfortable and spacious guest areas. Cozy up with a book in front of the original green stone fireplace. Or, help yourself to a variety of beverages or homemade treats from the bottomless cookie jar.

A full gourmet breakfast is served in the dramatic red dining room. House specialties include fresh seasonal fruit in champagne wine sauce, crème brûlée French toast and lemon soufflé pancakes with blueberries.

INNKEEPERS:	Becky Hodges and Dutch & Betty Schroeder
ADDRESS:	1910 Austin Avenue
	Waco, Texas 76701
TELEPHONE:	(254) 753-7294; (877) 632-2312
E-MAIL:	cotnpalace@aol.com
WEBSITE:	www.thecottonpalace.com
ROOMS:	4 Rooms; 2 Suites; 1 Cottage; Private baths
CHILDREN:	Children age 12 and older welcome
ANIMALS:	Not allowed
HANDICAPPED:	Not handicapped accessible
DIETARY NEEDS:	Will accommodate guests' special dietary needs

Crisp Waffles

Makes 4 Servings

"There are hundreds of waffle recipes — believe me, I've tried them all — but these really are the best!" ~ Innkeeper, The Cotton Palace Bed & Breakfast

¾   cup flour
¼   cup cornstarch
½   teaspoon salt
½   teaspoon baking powder
¼   teaspoon baking soda
¾   cup buttermilk
¼   cup milk
6   tablespoons vegetable oil
1   large egg, separated
1   tablespoon sugar
½   teaspoon vanilla extract

Preheat oven to 200°F. Preheat a lightly greased waffle iron. Mix flour, cornstarch, salt, baking powder and baking soda in a medium bowl. Combine buttermilk, milk, oil and egg yolk in a small bowl; add to dry ingredients and whisk until just mixed.

In a clean bowl, beat egg white almost to soft peaks. Sprinkle in sugar; beat until peaks are firm and glossy. Beat in vanilla. Drop beaten egg white into batter in dollops. Gently fold in egg white with a rubber spatula until just incorporated. Spoon batter onto hot waffle iron; bake until crisp and nutty brown. Remove waffle and set it directly on the oven rack to keep it warm and crisp. Repeat with remaining batter. (To keep waffles crisp, do not stack them.) Serve with syrup.

Variations:

Cranberry Orange Waffles: Stir 2 teaspoons finely grated orange zest and ½ cup coarsely chopped dried cranberries into the batter.

Chocolate Chip Waffles: Stir ½ cup coarsely chopped chocolate chips or ½ cup mini chocolate chips into the batter.

Cornmeal Waffles: Substitute ½ cup cornmeal for ½ cup of the flour.

Bonita - A Stagecoach Stop

Stagecoach Stop B+B

B onita - A Stagecoach Stop is the ideal spot for travelers desiring a picturesque landscape in which to enjoy gardens of antique roses, herbs and native plants. A gourmet breakfast is served in the fragrant rose garden, on the breezy porches or in the cozy dining room of the main house.

Breakfast includes a variety of fresh fruit, homemade breads, eggs, potato pancakes, New Braunfels sausage and Swedish pancakes.

INNKEEPERS:	Bettina & Jeff Messinger
ADDRESS:	5441 FM 1102
	New Braunfels, Texas 78132
TELEPHONE:	(830) 620-9453
E-MAIL:	stagecoach@satx.rr.com
WEBSITE:	www.stagecoachbedandbreakfast.com
ROOMS:	4 Rooms; 1 Suite; 4 Cottages; Private baths
CHILDREN:	Welcome
ANIMALS:	Not allowed; Resident dog, cat & rabbits
HANDICAPPED:	Handicapped accessible
DIETARY NEEDS:	Will accommodate guests' special dietary needs

Yeast Waffles

Makes 6 to 8 Servings (12 to 16 Waffles)

Make the batter for these waffles the night before serving. "This is one of our guests' favorites. It's best made with a Belgian waffle maker. I sometimes add fresh strawberries, whipped cream and chopped pecans." ~ Innkeeper, Bonita - A Stagecoach Stop

1	envelope (2½ teaspoons) active dry yeast
¼	cup warm water (105-115°F)
1	teaspoon plus 1 tablespoon sugar
2	cups warm milk (105-115°F)
1	stick (½ cup) butter, melted
2	cups flour
¼	teaspoon salt
2	eggs, lightly beaten
¼	teaspoon baking soda

Fresh strawberries, sliced (optional)
Whipped cream, for garnish (optional)
Chopped pecans, for garnish (optional)
Syrup, for serving

Stir the yeast into the warm water. Stir in 1 teaspoon of sugar. Let stand for 10 minutes (if the mixture foams and grows in volume, the yeast is active and ready to use).

Pour the warm milk into a large bowl. Add melted butter, flour, salt and 1 tablespoon of sugar; stir thoroughly. Stir in the yeast mixture. Put the batter into a large container with a tight fitting lid (the batter will double in size – be sure the container is large enough). Leave the container on the counter overnight.

The next morning, stir in the eggs and baking soda. Bake the waffles in a preheated, lightly greased waffle iron. Top with strawberries, whipped cream and pecans, if desired. Serve with syrup.

French Toast & Bread Pudding

French Toast
&
Bread Pudding

The Woodbine Hotel

Built in 1904, the Woodbine Hotel & Restaurant was originally the Shapira Hotel. The hotel offered accommodations for eight guests. Reinhard and Susan Warmuth purchased the Woodbine in 1999. Their goal is to return the hotel to its glory days when it was the town's social center and had the finest restaurant in the area. They hope that travelers will once again remark, as Norman Kittrel did in 1921: "There is not a hotel in Texas today, barring none, that ever served such meals as were served in that interior hamlet (of Madisonville)."

INNKEEPERS:	Chef Reinhard & Susan Warmuth
ADDRESS:	209 North Madison
	Madisonville, Texas 77864
TELEPHONE:	(936) 348-3333
E-MAIL:	woodbinehotel@aol.com
WEBSITE:	www.woodbinehotel.com
ROOMS:	8 Rooms; Private baths
CHILDREN:	Call ahead
ANIMALS:	Not allowed
HANDICAPPED:	Call ahead
DIETARY NEEDS:	Will accommodate guests' special dietary needs

Pecan-Crusted French Toast Filled with Maple Cream Cheese

Makes 4 Servings

8   eggs
2   tablespoons plus ¼ teaspoon vanilla
2   tablespoons cinnamon
½   cup sugar
2   pinches of salt, divided
8   ounces cream cheese, room temperature
¼   cup pure maple syrup
1   orange, juiced
8   slices Texas Toast bread
¾   pound medium-fine chopped pecans
¼   cup clarified butter (melted and skimmed unsalted butter)
Powdered sugar, fresh fruit and maple syrup, for garnish

Combine eggs, 2 tablespoons vanilla, cinnamon, sugar and a pinch of salt; whip until frothy and smooth. In a food processor, combine cream cheese, ¼ teaspoon vanilla, maple syrup, orange juice and a pinch of salt; blend until smooth.

Using an ice cream scoop, scoop 2 ounces of cream cheese into the middle of each of 4 slices of bread; do not spread – leave as a "ball" in the middle of the bread. (Variation: add sliced strawberries or blueberries or raspberries to the cream cheese). Top with remaining 4 slices of bread; press down gently so cream cheese lightly flattens but does not "squish out" of the sides. Place cream cheese sandwiches in egg mixture one at a time, lightly soaking both sides (don't get the bread too wet or the French toast will fall apart in the skillet). Place each sandwich in crushed pecans. Gently push down to "glue" pecans to battered bread, then turn and pecan crust the other side.

Heat clarified butter (whole butter will burn) in a very large skillet over medium heat. Cook sandwiches until golden brown on both sides. Remove from pan. Cut in half diagonally. Arrange 2 halves on each plate. Sprinkle with powdered sugar. Garnish with fresh fruit. Serve with warm maple syrup.

Rosevine Inn

Experience the old-fashioned concept of a bed and breakfast at the Rosevine Inn. Guest accommodations are cheerfully decorated, and each room has a private bath. The bed and breakfast is furnished with antiques and country collectibles.

The barn/game room is furnished in 1930's hunting lodge/tavern decor. A stone floor, fireplace, pub table, trophy heads and hides, and period furnishings complete the setting.

INNKEEPERS:	Rebecca & Bert Powell
ADDRESS:	415 South Vine
	Tyler, Texas 75702
TELEPHONE:	(903) 592-2221
EMAIL:	rosevine@iamerica.net
WEBSITE:	www.rosevine.com
ROOMS:	6 Rooms; 1 Suite; 2 Cottages; Private baths
CHILDREN:	Children age 5 and older welcome
ANIMALS:	Not allowed; Resident outdoor cats
HANDICAPPED:	Not handicapped accessible
DIETARY NEEDS:	Will accommodate guests' special dietary needs

Banana French Toast

Makes 2 to 4 Servings

"A serving is one 'sandwich,' but this is usually too much! So I cut them in half and let my guests decide." ~ Innkeeper, Rosevine Inn Bed & Breakfast

4	eggs
⅓	cup milk
1½	teaspoons cinnamon
1	tablespoon butter
4	slices multi-grain bread
2	ripe bananas, peeled and sliced lengthwise
½	cup maple syrup

Powdered sugar, for serving

Beat together eggs, milk and cinnamon in a shallow bowl. Melt butter in a large skillet over medium heat. Dip 2 pieces of bread in the egg mixture, coating each side. Place the 2 dipped slices in the skillet. Place bananas on top of the bread. Dip the remaining 2 slices of bread in the egg mixture and place on top of the slices in the skillet to make two "sandwiches." Cook on both sides until browned and cooked thoroughly.

Put French toast on warmed plates. Remove pan from heat and pour syrup in pan for 15 seconds to warm it. Pour warmed syrup over sandwiches, dust with powdered sugar and serve.

Pelican House

The Pelican House Bed & Breakfast, which was voted "Best of the Bay 2002," is located in a 90-year-old home situated on over an acre of property surrounded by live oak and pecan trees. There are wonderful views of the back bay from the front porch and from two of the rooms.

The Sunday specialty at the Pelican House is stuffed French toast with apricot glaze (see facing recipe), peppered bacon and fresh fruit.

INNKEEPERS:	Suzanne Silver
ADDRESS:	1302 First Street
	Seabrook, Texas 77586
TELEPHONE:	(281) 474-5295
E-MAIL:	pelicanhouse@usa.net
WEBSITE:	www.pelicanhouse.com
ROOMS:	4 Rooms; Private baths
CHILDREN:	Children age 10 and older welcome
ANIMALS:	Not allowed
HANDICAPPED:	Not handicapped accessible
DIETARY NEEDS:	Will accommodate guests' special dietary needs

Stuffed French Toast with Apricot Glaze

Makes 8 Servings

6	eggs
1	cup whole milk
1	teaspoon ground ginger
1	teaspoon cinnamon
1	teaspoon vanilla extract
1	(8-ounce) package cream cheese, room temperature
¼	cup chopped pecans
1	(8-ounce) can crushed pineapple, undrained
2	tablespoons apricot preserves
1	teaspoon almond extract
1	loaf French bread, cut into 1-inch thick slices (about 15-16 slices)

Butter, about 2 tablespoons

Apricot glaze:

¼	cup orange juice
¾	cup apricot preserves

Preheat oven to 350°F. Beat eggs, milk, ginger, cinnamon and vanilla in a large bowl. In another bowl, beat cream cheese until smooth. Add pecans, pineapple, apricot preserves and almond extract; mix well.

With the point of a sharp knife, make a slit in the center of the top crust in each slice of bread, cutting down a couple inches to make a "pocket." Stuff about 1 heaping tablespoon of the cream cheese mixture into each pocket. Soak bread in the egg mixture, thoroughly coating both sides. Cook in melted butter in a large skillet until bread is light brown on both sides. Put French toast on a lightly greased baking sheet. Bake for about 10 minutes, until heated through.

For the apricot glaze: Put apricot preserves and orange juice in a small saucepan over medium heat. Bring to a boil. Let boil until mixture is thickened and has a syrup consistency. Pour over the French toast to serve.

Mariposa Ranch

Mariposa Ranch Bed & Breakfast is located on a 100-acre working ranch along the historic La Bahia Trail. Accommodations include an 1870 plantation home, an 1820 log cabin, a quaint cottage, an 1836 Greek Revival home, a turn-of-the-century Texas farmhouse (the original homestead on this working ranch), a ranch hand's bunkhouse, a cozy settler's cottage and a real cowboy cabin.

Breakfast includes such treats as Texas Ranger baked eggs, Hill Country baked apples with lemon cream sauce, and German peach kuchen.

INNKEEPERS:	Johnna & Charles Chamberlain
ADDRESS:	8904 Mariposa Lane
	Brenham, Texas 77833
TELEPHONE:	(979) 836-4737; (877) 647-4774
E-MAIL:	info@mariposaranch.com
WEBSITE:	www.mariposaranch.com
ROOMS:	4 Rooms; 2 Suites; 5 Cottages; Private baths
CHILDREN:	Welcome
ANIMALS:	Not allowed; Resident cat & dogs
HANDICAPPED:	Not handicapped accessible
DIETARY NEEDS:	Will accommodate guests' special dietary needs

Orange Pecan French Toast

Makes 4 to 6 Servings

This is a very flavorful French toast, and it makes a beautiful presentation. Start the preparation for this dish the night before serving.

4	eggs
2/3	cup orange juice
1/3	cup milk
1/4	cup sugar
1/4	teaspoon nutmeg
1/4	teaspoon vanilla
1/4	cup Triple Sec (orange-flavored liqueur)
12	(1-inch thick) slices French bread
1/3	cup butter, melted
2	tablespoons grated orange zest
1/2	cup pecan pieces

Maple syrup, for serving

Mix eggs, orange juice, milk, sugar, nutmeg, vanilla and Triple Sec in a medium bowl. Dip each bread slice in the egg mixture, coating each side (do not soak) and place in a single layer on an ungreased 10x15-inch (or larger) jelly-roll pan or rimmed baking sheet. If there is any remaining egg mixture, pour it over the French toast in the pan. Cover and refrigerate overnight.

Preheat oven to 400°F. Spray a baking sheet with nonstick cooking spray. Arrange soaked bread slices in a single layer on the baking sheet. Drizzle melted butter over bread slices. Sprinkle with orange zest. Top with pecan pieces. Bake for 30-40 minutes, or until golden brown. Serve with syrup.

Terralak

Located about one hour north of Dallas, Terralak Bed & Breakfast is a five-bedroom, three-story house on 13 wooded acres overlooking the shores of beautiful Lake Texoma. The name "Terralak" was derived by combining "terra" (the land) with the first letter of the first name of each of the innkeeper's three daughters – Lindsey, Ashley and Kristen.

The Texas-size Master Suite features a spiral staircase leading to the Skyroom, which sits 40 feet above the ground and offers panoramic views of the lake.

INNKEEPERS:	Kathy Murray
ADDRESS:	2661 Tanglewood Drive
	Pottsboro, Texas 75076
TELEPHONE:	(903) 786-6335
EMAIL:	terralak@aol.com
WEBSITE:	www.terralak.com
ROOMS:	5 Rooms; Private baths
CHILDREN:	Welcome; Call ahead
ANIMALS:	Not allowed
HANDICAPPED:	Not handicapped accessible
DIETARY NEEDS:	Will accommodate guests' special dietary needs

Texas French Toast

Makes 6 Servings

"A true 'Texas-size' breakfast using Texas Toast and only the finest fresh Texas pecans. Serve with fresh fruit, bacon or ham, juice and coffee." - Innkeeper, Terralak Bed & Breakfast

6	large eggs
½	cup whole milk
1	tablespoon vanilla extract

Butter, for cooking

12	slices Texas Toast bread (it's 1-inch thick and sold in most groceries)
1	tablespoon powdered sugar
5	medium bananas, sliced
1	tablespoon cinnamon
2	cups fresh whole pecans, toasted

Maple syrup, for serving

Beat eggs, milk and vanilla together in a large bowl. Melt butter in a large skillet or on a griddle over medium-high heat. Dip Texas Toast in egg batter, coating both sides. Cook, turning once to brown both sides.

To serve, put French toast on a large platter and sprinkle with powdered sugar, sliced bananas, cinnamon and pecans. Serve with warm maple syrup.

Historic Moses Hughes Ranch

1856

The story of the Moses Hughes Ranch is one of love and hope, health and happiness. Moses Hughes and his wife, Hanna, who had been ill, were living in Georgetown, Texas when Moses heard stories from local Native Americans about springs with healthful properties in the heart of Texas. He packed up Hanna and their two children and brought them to Lampasas. After Hanna's health dramatically improved, they decided to make Lampasas their home and began building the ranch in 1853. Hanna lived to have 10 more children.

INNKEEPERS:	Al & Beverly Solomon
ADDRESS:	7075 West FM 580
	Lampasas, Texas 76550
TELEPHONE:	(512) 556-5923
E-MAIL:	mhrbb@n-link.com
WEBSITE:	www.moseshughesranch.com
ROOMS:	3 Rooms; Private baths
CHILDREN:	Children age 15 and older welcome
ANIMALS:	Not allowed; Resident outdoor cats
HANDICAPPED:	Not handicapped accessible
DIETARY NEEDS:	Will accommodate guests' special dietary needs

Orange Tarragon Croissant French Toast

Makes 4 Servings

"This is the most requested breakfast by my regular guests." ~ Innkeeper, Historic Moses Hughes Ranch Bed & Breakfast. This French toast needs to be started the night before serving.

4   eggs
⅔   cup orange juice
½   cup milk
¼   cup sugar
½   teaspoon vanilla extract
¼   teaspoon nutmeg
¼   teaspoon cinnamon
½   teaspoon dried tarragon
4   cold croissants, cut in half lengthwise
½   stick (¼ cup) butter, melted
Powdered sugar, for garnish
Fresh tarragon sprigs or rose buds, for garnish
Maple syrup, for serving

The night before serving, spray two 7x11-inch glass baking dishes with nonstick cooking spray. In a medium bowl, whisk together eggs, orange juice, milk, sugar, vanilla, nutmeg, cinnamon and tarragon. Put 4 croissant halves tightly into each baking dish. Pour the egg mixture over the croissant halves. Cover and refrigerate overnight.

The next morning, preheat oven to 400°F. Pour melted butter evenly over the croissants. Bake, uncovered, for 30 minutes. To serve, place 2 croissant halves on each of 4 plates. Sprinkle with powdered sugar and garnish with a fresh tarragon sprig or a rose bud. Serve with maple syrup.

Brava House

B uilt in the late 1880's, the Brava House was one of Austin's first Victorian homes. The structure has been lovingly restored and features elegant antique furnishings and charming architectural details including hardwood floors, high ceilings, crown molding and original fireplaces.

The Brava House is located just minutes from 6th Street, the Texas State Capitol, the University of Texas, the convention center, the Texas State History Museum, Barton Springs and the LBJ Library.

INNKEEPERS:	Shelley Seale
ADDRESS:	1108 Blanco Street
	Austin, Texas 78703
TELEPHONE:	(888) 545-8200
E-MAIL:	shelley@bravahouse.com
WEBSITE:	www.bravahouse.com
ROOMS:	2 Rooms; 2 Suites; Private baths
CHILDREN:	Welcome
ANIMALS:	Welcome; Resident dog
HANDICAPPED:	Handicapped accessible
DIETARY NEEDS:	Will accommodate guests' special dietary needs

Pecan-Crusted French Toast

Makes 6 Servings

"The pecans are what make this dish stand out as a real treat!" ~ Innkeeper, Brava House Bed & Breakfast Inn

3	eggs
½	cup milk
2	tablespoons orange juice
1	teaspoon cinnamon

Butter, for skillet or griddle

12	slices (small in diameter) French bread
½	cup chopped pecans

Orange slices, for garnish
Maple syrup, for serving

Beat eggs, milk, orange juice and cinnamon in a medium bowl. Melt butter on a griddle or in a skillet over medium heat. Dip each piece of bread lightly in the egg mixture, coating both sides, and place on the griddle. Sprinkle and press the pecans into the uncooked side of the bread. Turn bread over to brown both sides.

Serve the French toast pecan-side-up, two slices per person. Garnish each serving with a slice of orange. Serve with maple syrup on the side.

Crystal River Inn

If your travels take you anywhere near Austin or San Antonio, don't miss the Crystal River Inn, one of the oldest and most famous bed and breakfast/country inns in Texas. The inn is located in beautiful San Marcos, one of the crown jewels of the Hill Country. Just over two hours from Houston, the bustling little riverside town of San Marcos is surrounded by scenery that is among the best in Texas. San Marcos is home to nature theme parks, world-class shopping, whitewater sports, picturesque historic districts, merry festivals, great antiquing, wineries, theater and fine dining.

INNKEEPERS:	Mike, Cathy & Sarah Dillon
ADDRESS:	326 West Hopkins
	San Marcos, Texas 78666
TELEPHONE:	(512) 396-3739; (888) 396-3739
E-MAIL:	info@crystalriverinn.com
WEBSITE:	www.crystalriverinn.com
ROOMS:	12 Rooms; 3 Suites; Private baths
CHILDREN:	Welcome
ANIMALS:	Call ahead
HANDICAPPED:	Call ahead
DIETARY NEEDS:	Will accommodate guests' special dietary needs

Caramelized Upside-Down Breakfast Pudding

Makes 6 to 8 Servings

"This heavenly concoction is a variation on make-ahead baked French toast. It is a cross between sticky buns and fluffy custard – fabulous for special brunches." ~ Innkeeper, Crystal River Inn. This dish needs to be started the night before serving.

1½   sticks (¾ cup) butter, melted
2   cups packed brown sugar
½   teaspoon cinnamon
½   cup raisins (or chopped almonds)
6-8   slices (1½-2 inches thick) French or Italian bread
6   eggs
2   cups milk
1½   teaspoons vanilla extract
½   teaspoon ground nutmeg
Maple syrup, for serving (optional)

Combine melted butter, brown sugar and cinnamon; spread evenly into the bottom of a 9x13-inch baking dish. Sprinkle with raisins or almonds. Lay slices of bread on top (slices may be trimmed or squeezed slightly to fit the dish, if necessary). Whisk together eggs, milk, vanilla and nutmeg; pour evenly over the bread. Cover and refrigerate overnight.

The next morning, preheat oven to 350°F. Bake for 35-40 minutes, or until puffed and golden. Serve pieces of the pudding with the syrup from the bottom of the baking dish spooned over the top of each portion. Maple syrup is usually not necessary, but may be offered on the side.

Lazy Oak

Bed and Breakfast

Breakfast at the Lazy Oak consists of a vegetarian baked egg dish, large fruit bowl, homemade baked goods and pastries, bacon or ham, yogurt, granola, juices, cereals and breads. Sweets are left on the buffet in the afternoon and evening.

The Lazy Oak is available for use as a retreat. The innkeepers believe that the house has a special, restful energy and encourage small groups who want to come for a "re-charging."

INNKEEPERS:	Renee & Kevin Buck
ADDRESS:	211 West Live Oak Street
	Austin, Texas 78704
TELEPHONE:	(512) 447-8873; (877) 947-8873
E-MAIL:	lazyoakinn@aol.com
WEBSITE:	www.lazyoakbandb.com
ROOMS:	5 Rooms; Private baths
CHILDREN:	Children age 15 and older welcome
ANIMALS:	Not allowed; Resident dog
HANDICAPPED:	Not handicapped accessible
DIETARY NEEDS:	Will accommodate guests' special dietary needs

Raspberry Granola Bread Pudding

Makes 6 to 8 Servings

"This baked granola treat is perfect for cold mornings. If desired, it can be prepared the night before serving." ~ Innkeeper, Lazy Oak Bed & Breakfast

1	egg
¼	cup sugar
1½	cups milk
3-5	tablespoons butter, melted
1	cup fresh or frozen raspberries (or substitute blueberries)
3	cups granola

Maple syrup, for serving

Preheat oven to 350°F. Spray a 9-inch round or square baking pan with nonstick cooking spray. Beat together egg, sugar, milk and butter. Stir in raspberries and granola. Bake for 45-60 minutes, or until set. Serve with maple syrup.

Note: This is also good served later in the day with ice cream.

Karbach Haus

Guests of the Karbach Haus experience the *gemutlichkeit* (warm hospitality) of a German *gastehaus* with the amenities of a romantic, upscale resort. Stately and casually elegant, this historic home boasts turn-of-the-century ambiance with 20th-century comforts. A German-style breakfast is served each morning in the sun parlor or the formal dining room.

The Doctor's Suite is spacious and sunny. It is furnished with antique, Texas hand-made furniture, including an old, walnut, queen-size four-poster bed.

INNKEEPERS:	Kathy & Ben Jack Kinney
ADDRESS:	487 West San Antonio Street
	New Braunfels, Texas 78130
TELEPHONE:	(830) 625-2131; (800) 972-5941
E-MAIL:	khausbnb@aol.com
WEBSITE:	www.karbachhaus.com
ROOMS:	4 Rooms; 2 Suites; Private baths
CHILDREN:	Not allowed
ANIMALS:	Not allowed
HANDICAPPED:	Not handicapped accessible
DIETARY NEEDS:	Will accommodate guests' special dietary needs

Bread Pudding with Kahlúa Sauce

Makes 12 to 14 Generous Servings

1   (8-ounce) package plus 1 (3-ounce) package cream cheese, room temperature
1   cup plus ½ cup sugar
½   teaspoon vanilla extract
1   teaspoon cinnamon
12   slices day-old bread (we like Earth Grains San Francisco sourdough)
12   eggs
2   cups milk
½   teaspoon salt
½   stick (¼ cup) butter, melted and cooled
½   cup chopped pecans
Kahlúa sauce (recipe follows)
Whipped cream and/or powdered sugar, for serving

Butter a 9x13-inch baking pan. Cream together 8 ounces cream cheese, 1 cup sugar, vanilla and cinnamon. Spread mixture on 6 slices of bread. Sandwich with remaining 6 slices of bread. Cut or tear sandwiches into bite-size squares and pile them into baking pan. Beat eggs until light and fluffy. Add milk, the remaining 3 ounces of cream cheese, ½ cup sugar and salt; blend well. Pour over bread pieces. Cover and refrigerate overnight.

The next morning, preheat oven to 350°F. Brush top of bread pudding lightly with melted butter. Sprinkle with chopped pecans. Bake for 1 hour. Cool slightly on a wire rack. Serve warm with Kahlúa sauce, sweetened whipped cream and/or powdered sugar. (Note: This is good cold, too!)

Kahlúa sauce:
1   cup sour cream
1   cup brown sugar
1   cup whipped cream or non-dairy topping
½   teaspoon vanilla extract
¼   cup Kahlúa (or anywhere from 2-4 tablespoons, to your taste)

Thoroughly mix all ingredients together. Cover and refrigerate until ready to use. Stir again just before serving, as the Kahlúa tends to separate.

The Lodges at Lost Maples

From the sounds of gentle breezes rustling the leaves to the breathtaking views, the Lodges at Lost Maples is truly the ultimate hill country retreat. The inn is located in an area known as the "Swiss Alps of Texas." The rugged terrain and elevations as high as 2,100 feet above sea level make this area popular with recreational motorcyclists and bicyclists, as well as those who enjoy sightseeing. So, whether you are looking for a romantic getaway or a fun-packed family vacation, the Lodges at Lost Maples has something for everyone!

INNKEEPERS:	The Hathorn Family
ADDRESS:	77 Lower Sabinal River Road
	Vanderpool, Texas 78885
TELEPHONE:	(830) 966-5178; (877) 216-5627
E-MAIL:	lodges@lostmaplescabins.com
WEBSITE:	www.lostmaplescabins.com
ROOMS:	5 Cabins; Private baths
CHILDREN:	Welcome
ANIMALS:	Not allowed
HANDICAPPED:	Not handicapped accessible
DIETARY NEEDS:	Will accommodate guests' special dietary needs

The Lodges Rustic Chocolate Bread Pudding

Makes 12 Servings

"These are individual servings of chocolate bread pudding with a warm surprise in the center." ~ Innkeeper, The Lodges at Lost Maples

2	tablespoons butter
½	cup milk chocolate chips
½	cup packed brown sugar
2	eggs, slightly beaten
¼	teaspoon cinnamon
½	teaspoon vanilla extract
1½	cups heavy cream
½	cup milk
3	cups day-old bread cubes
3	(1-ounce) squares dark or semisweet chocolate

Powdered sugar, for garnish

Preheat oven to 350°F. Spray 12 muffin cups with nonstick cooking spray. In a microwave-safe bowl, melt butter and chocolate chips together in the microwave; stir well to combine. Whisk the brown sugar into the butter mixture. Add eggs, cinnamon and vanilla; whisk until well blended. Add cream and milk; whisk until well blended. Gently fold in bread cubes until combined; let stand for 10-15 minutes to allow the mixture to absorb most of the liquid.

Divide the bread pudding mixture between the muffin cups. Cut each square of chocolate into 4 pieces. Push one chocolate piece into the middle of the mixture in each muffin cup.

Bake for 35 minutes, or until the bread pudding is set. Remove from the muffin cups and place in paper muffin liners, if desired, to serve. Serve warm, sprinkled with powdered sugar.

Bogart's on the Boulevard

Bogart's on the Boulevard is a truly beautiful home featuring six palatial guest suites. The home has three floors and is decorated with antiques, eclectic furnishings, crystal chandeliers, stained- and beveled-glass accents, and many unique accessories. Upon arrival you will be greeted with welcome treats of the host's choice.

Bogart's is a City of Houston Landmark and was included in the National Register of Historic Places in 1984.

INNKEEPERS:	Dwayne Fuller
ADDRESS:	1536 Heights Boulevard
	Houston, Texas 77008
TELEPHONE:	(713) 802-1281; (713) 864-2500
E-MAIL:	Bogarts@EV1.net
WEBSITE:	www.bogarts.org
ROOMS:	5 Rooms; 1 Suite; Private baths
CHILDREN:	Not allowed
ANIMALS:	Not allowed
HANDICAPPED:	Not handicapped accessible
DIETARY NEEDS:	Will accommodate guests' special dietary needs

"A Loaf of Bread and Thou" Pudding with Bogart's Cream

Makes 12 Servings

30   slices cinnamon bread, cut into cubes (about 2 pounds bread)
10   eggs
3   cups half & half
1   cup sugar
½   cup (4 ounces) vanilla extract
2   sticks (1 cup) unsalted butter, melted
2   tablespoons cinnamon (optional or to taste)
1⅓ cups (8 ounces) white chocolate chips
Bogart's Cream (recipe follows)

Preheat oven to 325°F. Spray a 10x15-inch baking dish with nonstick cooking spray. Place bread cubes in a very large bowl. In a large bowl, combine eggs, half & half, sugar, vanilla, melted butter and cinnamon; mix well. Pour egg mixture over bread cubes. Add the white chocolate chips; stir to combine. Pour the mixture into the baking dish.

Bake, uncovered, for 45-50 minutes or until a toothpick inserted in the center comes out clean. Serve hot topped with Bogart's Cream.

Bogart's Cream:
1   cup sour cream
2   tablespoons sugar
2   tablespoons vanilla extract
1   teaspoon cinnamon

Combine all of the ingredients in a medium bowl. If prepared in advance, refrigerate until ready to use.

Inn on the Square

Inn on the Square, located in historic downtown Georgetown, is on the second floor of the Booty Building, overlooking the Courthouse District and square. This beautifully restored 1890's landmark, a fine example of high Victorian architecture, is listed on the National Register of Historic Places.

Stained and leaded glass, fireplaces, wood floors and fine moldings accent the spacious inn. The enchanting rooftop terrace is a delightful spot for enjoying morning coffee or romancing under the stars.

INNKEEPERS:	Joella & Joel Broussard
ADDRESS:	104½ West Eighth Street
	Georgetown, Texas 78626
TELEPHONE:	(512) 868-2203; (888) 718-2221
E-MAIL:	jandjbroussard@aol.com
WEBSITE:	www.innonthesquare.net
ROOMS:	4 Rooms; Private baths
CHILDREN:	Children age 14 and older welcome
ANIMALS:	Not allowed
HANDICAPPED:	Not handicapped accessible
DIETARY NEEDS:	Will accommodate guests' special dietary needs

Peggy's Holiday Bread Pudding

Makes 8 Servings

"Peggy Beeman is our fabulous cook! This pudding is very rich and delicious, yet quick and easy. We often serve it with a breakfast entrée." ~ Innkeeper, Inn on the Square

2	sticks (1 cup) butter
3	eggs
2	cups sugar
8	slices raisin/cinnamon bread, cubed
1	(20-ounce) can crushed pineapple, undrained

Preheat oven to 350°F. Butter an 8x8-inch or 9x9-inch baking dish. Cream together butter, eggs and sugar in a large bowl. Add cubed bread and pineapple; stir to combine. Pour mixture into dish. Bake, uncovered, for 60 minutes. Serve warm or cold.

Note: This bread pudding keeps well in the refrigerator for up to 5 days.

River Run

A spacious front porch welcomes you to the River Run Bed & Breakfast Inn, a step into a relaxed country home filled with antiques and Texana memorabilia. In the living room, you will be greeted by a turn-of-the-century pharmacy counter, displaying the inn's collection of early medicine. In the morning, a full country breakfast will be waiting.

Guests can venture to the Guadalupe River or follow a nature trail to Town Creek where native plants and wildlife abound.

INNKEEPERS:	Ron & Jean Williamson
ADDRESS:	120 Francisco Lemos Street
	Kerrville, Texas 78028
TELEPHONE:	(830) 896-8353; (800) 460-7170
E-MAIL:	riverrun@ktc.com
WEBSITE:	www.riverrunbb.com
ROOMS:	4 Rooms; 2 Suites; Private baths
CHILDREN:	Children age 17 and older welcome
ANIMALS:	Not allowed
HANDICAPPED:	Handicapped accessible; 1 room
DIETARY NEEDS:	Will accommodate guests' special dietary needs

Mexican Bread Pudding

Makes 10 Servings

½   cup chopped dried apricots
1   stick I Can't Believe It's Not Butter!, melted
1   loaf French bread (cut into 2-inch cubes)
½   cup sugar
4   large eggs
2   cups milk
2   teaspoons vanilla extract
½   teaspoon salt
1   teaspoon cinnamon

Cajeta Sauce:
1   cup packed brown sugar
¼   cup apricot nectar
½   cup chopped pecans
½   cup flaked coconut
3   tablespoons apricot brandy

For the bread pudding: Preheat oven to 375°F. Put apricots in a microwave-safe bowl; cover with water. Microwave for 2 minutes; set aside. Pour ½ of the I Can't Believe It's Not Butter! into an 8x12-inch glass baking dish. Spread the bread cubes into the bottom of the dish. Bake for 15 minutes.

Cream sugar and remaining I Can't Believe It's Not Butter! in a large bowl. Beat in eggs, milk, vanilla and salt. Drain the apricots; discard the liquid. Sprinkle apricots over the bread cubes. Sprinkle with cinnamon. Evenly pour the egg mixture over the ingredients in the dish. Place the glass baking dish inside a larger metal baking pan. Fill the outer pan with ½ inch of water. Cover loosely with foil. Bake for 20 minutes. Remove foil and bake for 15-20 minutes more, or until a toothpick inserted in the center comes out clean. Remove from oven; cool on a wire rack for 20 minutes. To serve, spoon Cajeta Sauce over the top of the bread pudding.

For the Cajeta Sauce: Mix brown sugar and apricot nectar in a microwave-safe glass bowl. Microwave for 3 minutes. Stir in pecans and coconut. Microwave for 3 minutes more. Stir in apricot brandy.

Egg Dishes & Breakfast Entrées

Egg Dishes
&
Breakfast Entrées

Elizabeth's Garden

Sunny days and starlit nights are nearly constant visitors at Elizabeth's Garden Bed & Breakfast, especially during the wildflower-filled spring and crisp, energizing fall seasons. Fredericksburg's abundant charms make it truly deserving of its reputation as the "Jewel of the Texas Hill Country."

Breakfast is serious business at Elizabeth's Garden. Presented on vintage trays and served on antique china and crystal from the owners' private collection, you are assured that this is no ordinary breakfast!

INNKEEPERS:	Bob & Patsy Schlieter
ADDRESS:	412 West Austin
	Fredericksburg, Texas 78624
TELEPHONE:	(830) 990-2504
E-MAIL:	eliza@ktc.com
WEBSITE:	www.bbonline.com/tx/elizabeths
ROOMS:	2 Suites; Private baths
CHILDREN:	Not allowed
ANIMALS:	Not allowed
HANDICAPPED:	Not handicapped accessible
DIETARY NEEDS:	Cannot accommodate guests' special dietary needs

Huevos de Domingos

Makes 8 Servings

"Huevos de Domingos literally means 'Sunday eggs.' This is my favorite egg recipe to serve you know when! It is a delicious vegetarian dish. For carnivores, simply add ½ pound crumbled, browned and well-drained spicy breakfast sausage to the mixture before baking." - Innkeeper, Elizabeth's Garden Bed & Breakfast

2   tablespoons butter
½   cup chopped green, red and/or yellow bell peppers
½   cup chopped onion
2   cups (8 ounces) grated Monterey Jack cheese
⅓   cup flour
1   teaspoon baking powder
8   eggs
1   (8-ounce) container low-fat cottage cheese
1   (2½-ounce) can sliced black olives
2   (4-ounce) cans diced green chilies
Garlic powder, salt and pepper, to taste

Preheat oven to 375°F. Spray an 8- or 9-inch square baking pan or a deep-dish pie pan with nonstick cooking spray. Melt butter in a medium skillet over medium-low heat. Cook bell peppers and onions until soft, but not browned. In a small bowl, combine Monterey Jack cheese, flour and baking powder; set aside. In a large bowl, whisk together eggs, cottage cheese, olives, green chilies, garlic powder, salt and pepper. Combine the egg mixture, bell pepper mixture and flour mixture. Pour into the pan.

Bake for 45-60 minutes, or until slightly risen and lightly browned on top, and a toothpick inserted in the middle comes out clean. Let stand for 5 minutes before slicing and serving.

Note: Sliced Roma tomatoes placed on top during the last 15 minutes of baking is a colorful and delicious addition.

Seven Gables

The Seven Gables Bed & Breakfast is located just 100 miles east of Dallas off Interstate 30, in Mount Vernon, a Main Street city with over 50 historical homes and buildings, and nearby berry picking and nature trails. The inn hosts murder mystery dinners for groups of eight to sixteen, with several themes to choose from.

Four- and five-course meals are available to inn guests, along with dessert at night.

INNKEEPERS:	Donnie & Deborah Thomas
ADDRESS:	318 South Kaufman
	Mount Vernon, Texas 75457
TELEPHONE:	(903) 537-3391
E-MAIL:	sevengablesbb@hotmail.com
WEBSITE:	www.sevengablesbedandbreakfast.com
ROOMS:	2 Rooms; 1 Suite; 1 Cottage; Private baths
CHILDREN:	Children age 12 and older welcome
ANIMALS:	Not allowed; Resident dog
HANDICAPPED:	Not handicapped accessible
DIETARY NEEDS:	Will accommodate guests' special dietary needs

Southern-Style Eggs Benedict

Makes 4 Servings

"This dish, perfect for breakfast or brunch, has a beautiful presentation and is our guests' favorite. They are always amazed to find cornbread replacing the English muffin used in the typical Eggs Benedict. Serve with hash browns and a bowl of fruit." ~ Innkeeper, Seven Gables Bed & Breakfast

1   package plain cornbread mix, any brand (size varies from 6- to 8½-ounces)

Eggs (amount according to cornbread mix directions)

Milk (amount according to cornbread mix directions)

2   tablespoons butter

2   tablespoons flour

1⅓   cups milk

1½   cups (6 ounces) grated cheddar cheese, divided

⅓   cup mayonnaise

¼   teaspoon hot sauce

4   hard-boiled eggs, peeled and chopped

Salt and pepper, to taste

4   green onions tops, chopped

Real bacon bits

1   small Roma tomato, seeded and chopped

Make cornbread according to mix directions. Bake cornbread in a greased 8x8-inch baking pan. Melt butter in a medium saucepan over low heat. Add flour and cook for 1 minute, whisking constantly until smooth. Gradually add milk and cook over medium heat, whisking constantly, until mixture is thickened and bubbly. Stir in ¾ cup of cheese, mayonnaise, hot sauce, eggs and salt and pepper; continue cooking until cheese is melted.

Preheat oven to 350°F. Cut cornbread into 4 squares. Then cut each square in half horizontally. Place 2 halves on each of 4 oven-proof serving plates, with the top and bottom halves slightly overlapping. Spoon cheese sauce over cornbread, covering well. Sprinkle the cornbread on each plate with some of the remaining cheese, the green onions, bacon bits and tomatoes. Put each plate in the oven for about 2 minutes, just until the cheese melts.

Mariposa Ranch

During your days at the Mariposa Ranch, enjoy the small-town charm of Brenham and the many attractions throughout Washington County. Back at the ranch, enjoy the charming surroundings, including live oak trees, grand vistas, sumptuous breakfasts, massages, candlelight dinners and a crackling fire in the privacy of your room or cottage.

"A romantic and historic getaway with warm hospitality and country elegance." ~ *Southern Living*

INNKEEPERS:	Johnna & Charles Chamberlain
ADDRESS:	8904 Mariposa Lane
	Brenham, Texas 77833
TELEPHONE:	(979) 836-4737; (877) 647-4774
E-MAIL:	info@mariposaranch.com
WEBSITE:	www.mariposaranch.com
ROOMS:	4 Rooms; 2 Suites; 5 Cottages; Private baths
CHILDREN:	Welcome
ANIMALS:	Not allowed; Resident cat & dogs
HANDICAPPED:	Not handicapped accessible
DIETARY NEEDS:	Will accommodate guests' special dietary needs

Texas Oven Omelet

Makes 12 Servings

A breakfast entrée that tastes great and is very colorful to serve. The omelet can be prepared the night before and baked in the morning.

12	eggs
1	cup sour cream
2	green bell peppers, diced
1	(8-ounce) carton sliced fresh mushrooms
1	(15-ounce) can diced tomatoes, drained
1	(16-ounce) box Velveeta cheese, cubed
1	pound ham, chopped
½	stick (¼ cup) butter, cut into small pieces

Butter a 9x13-inch baking dish. Beat eggs and sour cream in a large bowl. Stir in the remaining ingredients; mix well. Pour mixture into baking dish. (At this point, the dish may be covered and refrigerated overnight.)

Preheat oven to 325°F. Bake for 60 minutes (an additional 10-15 minutes of baking time will be needed if the mixture was refrigerated overnight). Let stand for 10 minutes before serving.

Beauregard House

The quiet elegance of the King William Historic District of downtown San Antonio is where you will find the Beauregard House Bed & Breakfast Inn. Enjoy the beauty of this historic district from one of the two porches available for your relaxation.

Just one block from the Riverwalk and within easy walking distance to the Alamo and Convention Center, the Beauregard House is the perfect place for business travelers and vacationers alike.

INNKEEPERS:	Lisa & Al Fittipaldi
ADDRESS:	215 Beauregard Street
	San Antonio, Texas 78204
TELEPHONE:	(888) 667-0555
E-MAIL:	info@beauregardhouse.com
WEBSITE:	www.beauregardhouse.com
ROOMS:	6 Rooms; 2 Suites; Private baths
CHILDREN:	Children age 16 and older welcome
ANIMALS:	Not allowed; Resident dog
HANDICAPPED:	Not handicapped accessible
DIETARY NEEDS:	Will accommodate guests' special dietary needs

Beauregard House River Breakfast

Makes 4 Servings

A delightful Southern breakfast of creamy eggs and river trout. "Hot-smoked" salmon fillet (not "lox") would be a delicious substitute for the trout, if desired.

8   eggs
1   (1½-ounce) package smoked trout fillet, broken into ½-inch pieces
4   ounces cream cheese, room temperature, cut into ½-inch pieces
½   cup chopped green onions
1½   tablespoons chopped fresh dill (plus 4 sprigs for garnish)
Salt and pepper, to taste
2½   tablespoons butter

Beat eggs with a whisk in a large bowl. Add trout, cream cheese, green onions, chopped dill, salt and pepper; stir to mix.

Melt butter in a large skillet over medium heat. Add egg mixture; stir gently until eggs are set, but still moist, about 4 minutes. Divide eggs between 4 plates. Garnish each serving with a dill sprig.

A Beckmann Inn

The gourmet breakfast at A Beckmann Inn is served in the formal dining room with china, crystal and silver. Fresh ground coffee, specialty teas, uniquely blended fruit juices, an entrée, fresh fruit and coffee cake, muffins or pastries are all on the menu.

Be sure to save room for A Beckmann Inn's signature second course "breakfast dessert."

INNKEEPERS:	Betty Jo & Don Schwartz
ADDRESS:	222 East Guenther Street
	San Antonio, Texas 78204
TELEPHONE:	(210) 229-1449; (800) 945-1449
E-MAIL:	beckinn@swbell.net
WEBSITE:	www.beckmanninn.com
ROOMS:	5 Rooms; Private baths
CHILDREN:	Children age 12 and older welcome
ANIMALS:	Not allowed
HANDICAPPED:	Not handicapped accessible
DIETARY NEEDS:	Will accommodate guests' special dietary needs

Southern Cornbread & Egg Casserole

Makes 12 Servings

For a vegetarian casserole, substitute diced green pepper and onion for the ham.

1	cup yellow cornmeal
1	cup flour
¼	teaspoon baking soda
2	tablespoons sugar
1¼	cups buttermilk
1	egg plus 8 eggs
¾	cup diced cooked ham
1½	cups (6 ounces) cheddar or Swiss cheese
2	cups milk

Dash of Pickapeppa or Worcestershire sauce
Salt and pepper, to taste

Preheat oven to 375°F. Spray a 9-inch round baking pan with nonstick cooking spray. Put cornmeal, flour, baking soda, sugar, buttermilk and 1 egg into a mixing bowl; stir just until combined. Pour into the pan and bake for 25 minutes, or until a toothpick inserted in the center comes out clean. Allow cornbread to cool.

When the cornbread is cooled, crumble it into large chunks and put it in a 9x13-inch baking pan sprayed with nonstick cooking spray. Sprinkle the ham and cheese over the top.

Whisk or beat together 8 eggs, milk, Pickapeppa sauce, salt and pepper in a large bowl. Pour over the ingredients in the pan. Bake for 30 minutes, or until done. Let stand for 5 minutes before serving.

Wilderness Bed & Breakfast

Wilderness Bed & Breakfast is located in a quiet, wooded residential section of Bryan, only minutes from Texas A&M University, the George Bush Library and other attractions. A full breakfast includes freshly baked breads and muffins, seasonal fruits and substantial Texas-style fare.

Innkeepers Jim and Millie Carter retired after 33 years with the Department of State, where they served in Chile, Mexico, Burma, South Africa, Jamaica, Argentina, Japan and the Philippines.

INNKEEPERS:	Jim & Millie Carter
ADDRESS:	3200 Wilderness Road
	Bryan, Texas 77807
TELEPHONE:	(979) 779-0675, (866) 779-0675
E-MAIL:	wildernessbnb@cox-internet.com
WEBSITE:	http://pages.tca.net/JWCARTER/index.html
ROOMS:	3 Rooms; Private & shared baths
CHILDREN:	Children age 10 and older welcome
ANIMALS:	Not allowed; Resident dog
HANDICAPPED:	Not handicapped accessible
DIETARY NEEDS:	Will accommodate guests' special dietary needs

Wilderness Corn & Green Chile Casserole

Makes 12 Servings

3	cups small-curd cottage cheese
10	large eggs
2	cups sour cream
2	cups (8 ounces) grated cheddar cheese
3	green onions, chopped
1	(4-ounce) can mild green chiles
1	cup corn, well-drained
1	stick (½ cup) butter, melted
½	cup flour
1	teaspoon baking powder

Preheat oven to 350°F. Spray a 9x13-inch baking pan with nonstick cooking spray. In a large bowl, cream cottage cheese with a mixer. Gently beat in the eggs. Stir in sour cream, cheddar cheese, green onions, green chiles, corn and melted butter. In a small bowl, combine flour and baking powder; stir into the egg mixture. Pour the mixture into the baking pan.

Bake, uncovered, for 45-50 minutes. Let stand for 5-10 minutes before cutting into serving pieces.

Camp David

Camp David Bed & Breakfast offers the privacy of your own cottage along with a full gourmet breakfast brought to your door each morning. The cottages and Pecan Suite (in the main house) have English Country decor and are furnished with European and American antiques.

Most units have fully equipped kitchens, extra-large whirlpool tubs and gas log fireplaces. Front porches lined with rockers and bistro tables invite you to relax and enjoy the breezes from the pecan tree-shaded courtyard.

INNKEEPERS:	Molly & Bob Sagebiel
ADDRESS:	708 West Main
	Fredericksburg, Texas 78624
TELEPHONE:	(830) 997-7797
E-MAIL:	cottages@ktc.com
WEBSITE:	www.campdavidbb.com
ROOMS:	1 Suite; 5 Cottages; Private baths
CHILDREN:	Children age 12 and older welcome
ANIMALS:	Not allowed
HANDICAPPED:	Not handicapped accessible
DIETARY NEEDS:	Call ahead

Eggs Amanda

Makes 2 Servings

"Amanda is our younger daughter. Like many young women, she doesn't always eat a big breakfast. But the first time I served this, she almost ate the plate! It was her recommendation to add the bacon ... a delicious suggestion!" ~ Innkeeper, Camp David Bed & Breakfast

2   bolillo rolls (found in Mexican bakeries), or substitute crusty French bread sub rolls, unsliced
2   hard-boiled eggs, peeled and sliced
1½   cups white sauce (recipe follows)
Paprika
Chives, chopped (or substitute chopped green onions)
2-4 tablespoons cooked, chopped bacon

Preheat oven to 350°F. Lightly grease or spray the bottoms of 2 individual, oval, shallow gratin dishes. Slice a thin layer off the top of the rolls and remove the soft bread inside, leaving a "bread shell." Lay the slices of egg inside the shell, using 1 egg per roll.

Ladle 1-2 tablespoons of white sauce into each dish. Place stuffed roll on the sauce and ladle more sauce over the egg and roll. Sprinkle with paprika and chives. Top with chopped bacon. Bake for 30 minutes. Serve hot.

White sauce:
2   tablespoons butter
2   tablespoons flour
1½   cups whole milk or half & half
½   teaspoon cumin
Salt and pepper, to taste

Melt butter in a medium saucepan over low heat. Stir in flour; cook until bubbly, stirring occasionally. Remove from heat. Slowly whisk in the milk. Return to the stove and cook over low heat, stirring constantly until thickened. Stir in cumin, salt and pepper.

The Gazebo

The Gazebo Bed & Breakfast is a two-story, Georgian-style home designed and built by innkeepers Clyde and Janet McMurray in 1981. In the foyer, you will be greeted by a 20-foot ceiling and a beautiful French crystal chandelier. The antique-filled parlor and the elegant dining room each have a fireplace.

The innkeepers strive to offer guests comfort, privacy, relaxation and Southern hospitality in a small, rural, Texas Main Street town.

INNKEEPERS:	Clyde & Janet McMurry
ADDRESS:	906 Sessions Street
	Bowie, Texas 76230
TELEPHONE:	(940) 872-4852
E-MAIL:	gazebobnb@aol.com
WEBSITE:	www.gazebobnb.com
ROOMS:	4 Rooms; Private & shared baths
CHILDREN:	Children age 12 and older welcome
ANIMALS:	Not allowed; Resident cat
HANDICAPPED:	Not handicapped accessible
DIETARY NEEDS:	Will accommodate guests' special dietary needs

Mediterranean Egg Soufflé

Makes 4 Servings

"We serve this delicious egg dish as a double entrée with French toast or Belgian waffles, although it could easily be an entrée on its own. It always gets raves!" ~ Innkeeper, The Gazebo B&B. This dish needs to be refrigerated overnight.

2-3	slices white bread, crusts removed
2	tablespoons butter, melted
1	(3-ounce) package cream cheese, cut into small pieces
3	ounces feta cheese, crumbled
12	ounces ham, cubed
1½	cups (6 ounces) grated sharp cheddar cheese
¼	cup (2 ounces) grated mozzarella cheese
4	medium eggs, slightly beaten
½	cup half & half
1	teaspoon all-purpose Greek seasoning
1	teaspoon Coleman's dry mustard
1½	tablespoons chopped chives

Parsley sprigs for garnish

Spray an 8x8-inch baking dish with nonstick cooking spray. Tear bread into pieces and place in bottom of dish. Pour melted butter over bread. Sprinkle cream cheese pieces and crumbled feta cheese over bread. Sprinkle ham and then cheddar and mozzarella cheeses on top.

Combine eggs, half & half, Greek seasoning and dry mustard in a medium bowl. Beat until well mixed and pour evenly over the cheese. Sprinkle chives on top. Cover and refrigerate overnight.

The next morning, preheat oven to 350°F. Bake for 50-60 minutes, or until mixture is set. Let stand for 5 minutes before serving. Garnish each serving with a sprig of fresh parsley.

Elizabeth's Garden

The Sundance Suite at Elizabeth's Garden reflects the palate of nature's daylight colors. This three-room suite on the first floor is dressed in earthy greens, pale pinks and sunlit yellows. This grand retreat is furnished with 19th-century antiques and vintage lighting.

"The setting, the food and the tranquility here have been wonderful, very relaxing and very much appreciated. Thank you for allowing us to share this very special corner of the world." ~ Guest, Aberdeen, Scotland

INNKEEPERS:	Bob & Patsy Schlieter
ADDRESS:	412 West Austin
	Fredericksburg, Texas 78624
TELEPHONE:	(830) 990-2504
E-MAIL:	eliza@ktc.com
WEBSITE:	www.bbonline.com/tx/elizabeths
ROOMS:	2 Suites; Private baths
CHILDREN:	Not allowed
ANIMALS:	Not allowed
HANDICAPPED:	Not handicapped accessible
DIETARY NEEDS:	Cannot accommodate guests' special dietary needs

Eggs Elizabeth

Makes 4 to 6 Servings

"This is our signature breakfast entrée – easy to prepare, tasty and we liked the name! It can be assembled the night before, refrigerated and baked in the a.m. – every B&B owner's dream!" ~ *Innkeeper, Elizabeth's Garden Bed & Breakfast*

2	cups (8 ounces) grated Swiss cheese (Gruyère or Emmenthaler produces the most sublime flavor)
⅓	cup flour
1	teaspoon baking powder
½	(10-ounce) package chopped spinach, thawed and well drained
½	cup crumbled cooked bacon (about 5 slices), or diced cooked ham
8	eggs
½	cup low-fat or fat-free cottage cheese
½	cup half & half
⅛	teaspoon salt, or to taste
⅛	teaspoon pepper, or to taste
¼	teaspoon garlic powder, or to taste

Combine cheese, flour and baking powder in a large bowl. Combine remaining ingredients in a medium bowl; stir into the cheese mixture, then pour into well-greased, deep, individual ramekins (8-ounce capacity) for 4 servings, or custard cups (7-ounce capacity) for 6 servings. Fill cups to about ⅓-inch from the top (this allows room for the mixture to puff up without spilling over). Bake immediately or cover and refrigerate overnight.

Preheat oven to 350°F. Bake for 30-35 minutes, or until lightly browned and puffed, and a toothpick inserted in the center comes out clean. (If the mixture was refrigerated overnight, an additional 5 minutes of baking time might be needed.)

A Long Stay

Located on the southern edge of the beautiful Texas Hill Country, A Long Stay offers an ideal setting for your next quiet vacation, getaway or conference. You'll have such an enjoyable time soaking in the peaceful energy, you'll never want to leave.

The Black Beauty Room is just that – quite a beauty. The artwork and furnishings all work together to create the charm of Texas. The porcelain tub has brass claw feet and a matching classic showerhead.

INNKEEPERS:	Pat Long & Linda Long
ADDRESS:	137 Old San Antonio Road
	Boerne, Texas 78006
TELEPHONE:	(830) 249-1234; (877) 566-4782
E-MAIL:	longstay@gvtc.com
WEBSITE:	www.alongstay.com
ROOMS:	4 Rooms; 2 Suites; 1 Cottage; Private baths
CHILDREN:	Welcome
ANIMALS:	Small dogs allowed; Resident dog, goats & horse
HANDICAPPED:	Not handicapped accessible
DIETARY NEEDS:	Will accommodate guests' special dietary needs

Eggs Bel-Mar

Makes 6 Servings

"This recipe is loved by the 'Bikers' and 'Horse Ropers.' It can be assembled the night before and refrigerated. In the morning, let it stand at room temperature for 30 minutes before baking. We serve it with Sausage Blueberry Coffee Cake (see recipe on page 51)." ~ Innkeeper, A Long Stay

½   stick (¼ cup) butter plus 4 tablespoons butter, divided
¼   cup flour
2   cups milk
1   teaspoon salt
½   teaspoon pepper
1   (6-ounce) package ham or Canadian bacon, chopped
¼   cup chopped green pepper
¼   cup chopped green onion
½   pound fresh mushrooms, sliced
18   eggs, slightly beaten
1   cup soft bread crumbs
2   tablespoons butter, melted

Make a white sauce by melting ½ stick butter in a saucepan over low heat. Add flour; stir until smooth. Cook for 1 minute; stirring constantly. Gradually stir in the milk. Cook over medium heat, stirring constantly, until thickened and bubbly, about 10 minutes. Add salt and pepper; set aside.

Grease a 9x13-inch baking dish. Melt 2 tablespoons butter in a large skillet over medium heat. Cook ham, green pepper, green onion and mushrooms until vegetables are crisp-tender; drain liquid. Melt remaining 2 tablespoons of butter in another large skillet over medium-low heat. Add beaten eggs. Cook, without stirring, until mixture begins to set on the bottom. Draw a wooden or heat-proof rubber spatula across the bottom of the pan to form large curds. Continue in same manner (tilting pan to let uncooked egg run to bottom of pan) until eggs are thickened but still moist. Remove from heat. Gently stir in ham mixture and white sauce. Spoon into baking dish.

Preheat oven to 350°F. Combine bread crumbs and 2 tablespoons melted butter; stir well to combine. Sprinkle evenly over the egg mixture. Bake, uncovered, for 20-25 minutes, or until heated thoroughly.

Lazy Oak

The Lazy Oak Bed & Breakfast is a historic plantation-style farmhouse built in 1911 for the Sheltons, a prominent south Austin family who raised six sons in the house. The Lazy Oak is minutes from the Capitol, 6th Street, the convention center and the downtown business district.

The feel of the home is open, airy and relaxed, with a mix of antique and eclectic furnishings. Original art is shown throughout the house.

INNKEEPERS:	Renee & Kevin Buck
ADDRESS:	211 West Live Oak Street
	Austin, Texas 78704
TELEPHONE:	(512) 447-8873; (877) 947-8873
E-MAIL:	lazyoakinn@aol.com
WEBSITE:	www.lazyoakbandb.com
ROOMS:	5 Rooms; Private baths
CHILDREN:	Children age 15 and older welcome
ANIMALS:	Not allowed; Resident dog
HANDICAPPED:	Not handicapped accessible
DIETARY NEEDS:	Will accommodate guests' special dietary needs

Lazy Oak Egg Bake

Makes 8 Servings

"This is a perfect recipe for those on the high protein/low carb diet – no crust and lots of protein – and it can be prepared the night before." - Innkeeper, Lazy Oak Bed & Breakfast

1   (10-ounce) can Rotel tomatoes with green chiles, drained
2   cups (8 ounces) grated cheese of choice
Assorted vegetables, such as sliced squash or mushrooms, or chopped green or red bell peppers (optional)
12 eggs, beaten well
1   cup sour cream
Mrs. Dash or salt and pepper, to taste

Preheat oven to 350°F. Spray a 9-inch round or square baking pan with nonstick cooking spray. Pour drained tomatoes into pan. Sprinkle with grated cheese. Add vegetables, if desired.

Beat eggs in a large bowl. Add sour cream and seasonings; mix well. Pour egg mixture over ingredients in pan. Bake for 30-40 minutes, or until browned and firm in the middle. Let stand for 5 minutes before serving.

Seven Gables

The wrap-around porch at Seven Gables Bed & Breakfast is the perfect place to watch the sun come up. There you will find a peaceful swing and wicker furniture to recline in while waiting for a gourmet breakfast in the dining room.

Every room has thick, fluffy towels, Bath & Body Works products and monogrammed robes.

INNKEEPERS:	Donnie & Deborah Thomas
ADDRESS:	318 South Kaufman
	Mount Vernon, Texas 75457
TELEPHONE:	(903) 537-3391
E-MAIL:	sevengablesbb@hotmail.com
WEBSITE:	www.sevengablesbedandbreakfast.com
ROOMS:	2 Rooms; 1 Suite; 1 Cottage; Private baths
CHILDREN:	Children age 12 and older welcome
ANIMALS:	Not allowed; Resident dog
HANDICAPPED:	Not handicapped accessible
DIETARY NEEDS:	Will accommodate guests' special dietary needs

French Baked Eggs

Makes 1 Large Serving

"If you love onions, you will enjoy this dish. Serve with your favorite breakfast meat for a hearty meal." ~ Innkeeper, Seven Gables Bed & Breakfast

1-2	slices French bread (or white sandwich bread), trimmed to fit the bottom of an individual baking dish
4½	tablespoons butter, divided
½	cup diced onion
¼	cup water
1	beef bouillon cube (or 1 teaspoon instant bouillon granules)
2	eggs

White or black pepper, to taste
Grated cheddar cheese (enough to top the dish before baking)

Preheat oven 425°F. Spray a 1½-cup capacity baking dish with nonstick cooking spray (Seven Gables uses oval, but any shape will do). Melt 2 tablespoons of butter in a small nonstick skillet over medium heat. Place the "cut to fit" slice of bread in the skillet and brown on both sides. Place the bread in the baking dish.

In the same skillet, over medium heat, melt 2 more tablespoons of butter. Cook onions in butter until translucent and tender. Pour onions on top of the toasted bread. Heat water and bouillon cube in a microwave-safe bowl in the microwave (or in a small saucepan on the stove). Stir until bouillon is dissolved, then pour over the onions and toasted bread.

With the back of a spoon, make an indentation in the onion mixture. Crack the eggs and place them in the indentation so they sit evenly in the dish. Season with white or black pepper. Sprinkle cheese over the top. Dot with the remaining ½ tablespoon of butter. Bake for about 15 minutes, or until cheese is melted and eggs are set or done to your liking.

The Full Moon Inn

The Full Moon Inn is a historic 1860 property nestled on 12 manicured acres with six enchanting rooms rich with charm and class. The inn is a scenic one-hour drive from San Antonio or Austin, and just minutes from three wineries, two state parks, the Guadalupe River, the historic Luckenbach Dance Hall and great antiquing in Fredericksburg.

The Old Smokehouse Cottage, decorated with sunflowers, picket fence, barn wood and cozy comfort, was featured in *Southern Living's Texas Vacations*.

INNKEEPERS:	Captain Matthew Carinhas
ADDRESS:	3234 Luckenbach Road
	Fredericksburg, Texas 78624
TELEPHONE:	(830) 997-2205; (800) 997-1124
E-MAIL:	info@fullmooninn.com
WEBSITE:	www.fullmooninn.com
ROOMS:	5 Rooms; 1 Cabin; Private baths
CHILDREN:	Welcome
ANIMALS:	Call ahead; Resident pets
HANDICAPPED:	Handicapped accessible
DIETARY NEEDS:	Will accommodate guests' special dietary needs

Eggs Luckenbach

Makes 6 to 8 Servings

"We like to serve Eggs Luckenbach with French toast and German sausage. The eggs hold well on the stove top or in a warm oven while finishing up last-minute breakfast preparations." ~ Innkeeper, The Full Moon Inn

3	tablespoons bacon drippings (for the best flavor), or butter or canola oil
1	cup French's French fried onions
½	cup chopped green onions
12	eggs
2	tablespoons Louisiana hot sauce

Suggested garnishes: mint leaves, strawberries or chopped green onion tops

Heat bacon drippings in a 10-inch nonstick pan over medium heat. Cook French fried onions and green onions just until hot. Mix eggs and hot sauce in a blender on low speed (or beat thoroughly with a mixer or by hand); add to hot mixture in pan. Lower heat and scramble eggs until almost done, but still moist.

Using a wooden spatula, pat the eggs down until the mixture is smooth in the pan. Cover with a lid or foil. Turn off the heat and let stand on the burner or put the pan in a preheated 185°F oven for 5-6 minutes to set up. Cut into wedges to serve. Garnish as desired.

Star of Texas

The Wildrose Retreat at the Star of Texas is a little house built in 1908. The innkeepers moved the house to their property and restored it as a private retreat for guests of the inn. The house has a spacious sitting room, kitchenette and a large bath with a two-person Jacuzzi tub. A stairway leads to a loft bedroom with a queen-size iron bed.

Double French doors lead out to a sitting deck to enjoy the sunrise or a quiet evening under the stars.

INNKEEPERS:	Don & Debbie Morelock
ADDRESS:	650 Morelock Lane
	Brownwood, Texas 76801
TELEPHONE:	(800) 850-2003
E-MAIL:	relaxing@star-of-texas.com
WEBSITE:	www.star-of-texas.com
ROOMS:	1 Suite; 2 Cottages; Private baths
CHILDREN:	Not allowed
ANIMALS:	Call ahead; Resident pets
HANDICAPPED:	Not handicapped accessible
DIETARY NEEDS:	Will accommodate guests' special dietary needs

Rosemary Cream Cheese Eggs

Makes 2 Servings

"These eggs are so flavorful! Serve them with Canadian bacon and fresh fruit."
~ Innkeeper, Star of Texas Bed & Breakfast

4	**eggs**
¼	**cup cream**
3	**small sprigs fresh rosemary leaves, finely snipped (about 1 teaspoon, or to taste)**
3	**tablespoons cream cheese**

Salt and pepper, to taste

Beat eggs and cream with a whisk in a medium bowl; pour into a greased small skillet over medium-low heat. Add the rosemary. Soft scramble the eggs. Pinch off small pieces of cream cheese and add to the eggs. Gently stir to melt the cream cheese. Season with salt and pepper.

Serving suggestion: Divide the eggs between 2 plates. Accompany with colorful fresh fruit, breakfast meat of choice and muffins or toast.

Brava House

Known for its casual and playful nature, Austin is the "playground of Texas," and the gateway to the Texas Hill Country. As the state capitol and home to the University of Texas, the city supports a politically charged and culturally rich environment. An outdoor mecca, Austin is blessed with a temperate year-round climate and 300 days of sunshine a year.

Every Sunday, the Brava House Bed & Breakfast Inn hosts a Champagne Brunch, complete with mimosas and berries with cream.

INNKEEPERS:	Shelley Seale
ADDRESS:	1108 Blanco Street
	Austin, Texas 78703
TELEPHONE:	(888) 545-8200
E-MAIL:	shelley@bravahouse.com
WEBSITE:	www.bravahouse.com
ROOMS:	2 Rooms; 2 Suites; Private baths
CHILDREN:	Welcome
ANIMALS:	Welcome; Resident dog
HANDICAPPED:	Handicapped accessible
DIETARY NEEDS:	Will accommodate guests' special dietary needs

Egg Cups with Sun-Dried Tomatoes

Makes 6 Servings

"These are always a big hit with our guests!" ~ Innkeeper, Brava House Bed & Breakfast Inn

6	eggs
1	cup whole milk
1	teaspoon finely chopped fresh basil

Salt and pepper, to taste (about a pinch each)

| 6 | tablespoons chopped sun-dried tomatoes (drained, if oil-packed) |
| 6 | tablespoons crumbled feta cheese |

Preheat oven to 350°F. Spray 6 ramekins or deep custard cups (6-ounce capacity) with nonstick cooking spray. In a medium bowl, whisk together eggs, milk, basil, salt and pepper. Put 1 tablespoon sun-dried tomatoes and 1 tablespoon feta cheese into each ramekin. Divide the egg mixture between the ramekins (about ⅓ cup each).

Bake for about 30 minutes, or until puffed and a toothpick inserted in the center comes out clean.

Camp David

C onveniently located on far west Main Street, the Camp David Bed & Breakfast offers a charming collection of five cottages behind the main house. As with the original "Camp David," each cottage is named for a local tree. Fredericksburg boasts several award-winning wineries that you can visit to learn a bit about the art of winemaking and sample their wines.

"Thank you for an extremely enjoyable stay. Breakfast was scrumptious and your hospitality was engaging." ~ Guest, Camp David B&B

INNKEEPERS:	Molly & Bob Sagebiel
ADDRESS:	708 West Main
	Fredericksburg, Texas 78624
TELEPHONE:	(830) 997-7797
E-MAIL:	cottages@ktc.com
WEBSITE:	www.campdavidbb.com
ROOMS:	1 Suite; 5 Cottages; Private baths
CHILDREN:	Children age 12 and older welcome
ANIMALS:	Not allowed
HANDICAPPED:	Not handicapped accessible
DIETARY NEEDS:	Call ahead

Jason's Breakfast Chile Strata

Makes 8 Servings

Assemble this dish the night before serving. "Jason is our oldest child. He's always had a taste for things Tex-Mex, so I altered a standing recipe to use Mexican flavorings and cheeses. He approved. I always tell my guests that this is one of the easiest dishes in the world … and it smells wonderful while baking. It's good cold for lunch, too!" - Innkeeper, Camp David Bed & Breakfast

4	large or 8 small flour tortillas
1	(4-ounce) can chopped green chilies
1	cup (about) chopped cooked ham or Canadian bacon
2	cups (8 ounces) grated Monterey Jack cheese
2	cups (8 ounces) grated four cheese-blend, preferably Mexican blend
6	eggs
2	cups half & half
1	teaspoon adobo seasoning (or Mexican-style salt/seasoning blend)*
1	scant tablespoon dried cilantro

Picante sauce for serving

Spray a 9x13-inch baking pan with nonstick cooking spray. Line the bottom of the pan with ½ of the tortillas, cutting or tearing to fit (it need not be a completely solid layer, but try not to overlap the pieces). Spread ½ of the green chilies on top of the tortillas. Sprinkle ½ of the ham over the chilies. Sprinkle ½ of the cheeses over all. Repeat the layers, ending with the cheeses. Beat together eggs, half & half, adobo seasoning and cilantro; pour over the ingredients in the pan. Cover and refrigerate overnight.

The next morning, preheat oven to 350°F. Bake, uncovered, for 60 minutes. Let stand for 10 minutes before slicing. Serve with picante sauce served in individual mini-ramekins set alongside the strata.

*Note: Adobo seasoning is a traditional Mexican spice mix. It is not hot, but is spicy and rich in flavor. It is available from Penzeys Spices ((800) 741-7787/www.penzeys.com), where it is hand-mixed from garlic, onion, Tellicherry black pepper, Mexican oregano, cumin and cayenne pepper.

Seven Gables

Whether you want to escape the stress of the city or celebrate a special occasion, the Seven Gables Bed & Breakfast will cater to your every need. The Pillow Room is decorated with a soft pink and cream floral theme. The antique iron bed, with piles of pillows, invites you to relax and enjoy a restful night's sleep.

Mount Vernon has over 100 antique stores within a 30 minute drive.

INNKEEPERS:	Donnie & Deborah Thomas
ADDRESS:	318 South Kaufman
	Mount Vernon, Texas 75457
TELEPHONE:	(903) 537-3391
E-MAIL:	sevengablesbb@hotmail.com
WEBSITE:	www.sevengablesbedandbreakfast.com
ROOMS:	2 Rooms; 1 Suite; 1 Cottage; Private baths
CHILDREN:	Children age 12 and older welcome
ANIMALS:	Not allowed; Resident dog
HANDICAPPED:	Not handicapped accessible
DIETARY NEEDS:	Will accommodate guests' special dietary needs

Mushroom & Spinach Frittata

Makes 6 Servings

"This dish is perfect for breakfast or brunch — serve with sliced fresh tomatoes and fresh fruit." ~ Innkeeper, Seven Gables Bed & Breakfast

3	tablespoons butter
8	ounces fresh mushrooms, sliced
8	ounces fresh spinach leaves, chopped
8	eggs, beaten
¼	teaspoon salt
⅛	teaspoon pepper
1	cup sour cream
¼	cup finely chopped fresh parsley

Preheat oven to 400°F. Spray a 9-inch pie pan with nonstick cooking spray. Melt butter in a nonstick skillet over medium heat. Add mushrooms; cook until softened. Add spinach; cook until wilted. Put the mushroom/spinach mixture into the pie pan.

Beat eggs, salt and pepper; pour on top of the mushroom/spinach mixture and stir to combine. Bake for 20 minutes, or until a toothpick inserted in the center comes out clean (be careful not to overcook).

While the frittata is baking, combine sour cream and parsley in a small bowl. Stir to mix and refrigerate until the frittata is done baking. To serve, slice the frittata into wedges. Garnish with a spoonful of the sour cream/parsley mixture.

Elizabeth's Garden

Elizabeth's Garden Bed & Breakfast is located on a century-old German homestead nestled in the heart of Fredericksburg's prestigious historic district. The inn is surrounded by towering pecan trees planted by the early German settlers. This "garden" setting is just a block from Main Street's antique shops, boutiques, museums and restaurants.

The Stardust Suite features a secluded treetop deck with a swing and dining area, a romantic and serene loft, and a dressing area with an antique vanity.

INNKEEPERS:	Bob & Patsy Schlieter
ADDRESS:	412 West Austin
	Fredericksburg, Texas 78624
TELEPHONE:	(830) 990-2504
E-MAIL:	eliza@ktc.com
WEBSITE:	www.bbonline.com/tx/elizabeths
ROOMS:	2 Suites; Private baths
CHILDREN:	Not allowed
ANIMALS:	Not allowed
HANDICAPPED:	Not handicapped accessible
DIETARY NEEDS:	Cannot accommodate guests' special dietary needs

Patsy's Hill Country Scramble

Makes 4 Servings

"This breakfast entrée evolved as a way to incorporate some of the many locally grown organic veggies available at our Farmer's Market! Rich, but heavenly – it always gets rave reviews." ~ Innkeeper, Elizabeth's Garden Bed & Breakfast

2	tablespoons butter
1	clove garlic, minced
⅓	cup finely chopped green onion
⅓	cup chopped green, red and/or yellow bell peppers
1	(3-ounce) package original Philadelphia cream cheese, cubed
⅓	cup heavy cream
½	cup crumbled crisp-cooked bacon
6	extra-large eggs

Salt and pepper, to taste
Italian seasoning, to taste

4	English muffins

Grated cheddar cheese, for garnish
Fresh or dried dill, for garnish

Melt butter in a large skillet over medium-low heat. Add garlic, onion and peppers; cook until soft (do not brown). Add cream cheese and heavy cream. Stir until melted and blended (do not let the mixture boil). Add bacon and stir. Whisk eggs, salt, pepper and Italian seasoning in a bowl; add to the skillet. Scramble the entire mixture into creamy soft curds (be careful not to overcook).

Split and lightly toast the English muffins. Place 2 English muffin halves on each plate. Top each muffin half with a generous scoop of the egg mixture. Garnish with a sprinkle of cheddar cheese and a sprinkle of dill.

The Columns on Alamo

The Rockhouse Cottage at the the Columns on Alamo is a small, 1881-style limestone house set back amongst the trees. The decor celebrates the Texas cowboy heritage with comfortable rustic pine furniture and historic photos of cowboys at work and play.

Ellenor and Art Link are resident innkeepers who can suggest excursion itineraries, dining and shopping adventures, and cultural and seasonal events unique to San Antonio.

INNKEEPERS:	Ellenor & Art Link
ADDRESS:	1037 South Alamo
	San Antonio, Texas 78210
TELEPHONE:	(210) 271-3245; (800) 233-3364
E-MAIL:	artlink@columnssanantonio.com
WEBSITE:	www.columnssanantonio.com
ROOMS:	13 Rooms; 1 Cottage; Private baths
CHILDREN:	Welcome
ANIMALS:	Not allowed
HANDICAPPED:	Not handicapped accessible
DIETARY NEEDS:	Will accommodate guests' special dietary needs

Texas Quiche

Makes 6 Servings

Green chilies, Tabasco sauce, black pepper and salsa add a kick to this dish. "A quiche designed for 'real men.'" ~ Innkeeper, The Columns on Alamo

1   (9-inch) deep-dish pie crust, unbaked (thawed, if frozen)
1½ cups (6 ounces) grated colby or Monterey Jack cheese
1   (4-ounce) can chopped green chilies, drained
3   eggs
1½ cups heavy cream
3   dashes Tabasco sauce
Black pepper, to taste
Red or green salsa, for serving

Preheat oven to 350°F. Layer the cheese, then the chilies into the bottom of the crust. Beat together eggs, cream, Tabasco and pepper. Pour the egg mixture over the cheese and chilies – *do not stir!* Bake for 35-40 minutes, or until browned and a toothpick inserted in center comes out clean. Serve hot, with salsa on the side.

Fair Breeze Cabin

Fair Breeze Cabin is located on Old Spanish Bluff Road, bordering Bonaldo Creek in Historic Nacogdoches County. Rustic in nature, the cabin is surrounded by walnut trees and overlooks 46 pastoral acres. The quiet setting offers a peaceful retreat to guests desiring an escape to the country for a relaxing weekend.

The cabin is located eight miles from Nacogdoches. If you like fun shopping and quaint restaurants, you'll absolutely love visiting the oldest town in Texas!

INNKEEPERS:	Stan & Christie Cook
ADDRESS:	4741 County Road 724
	Nacogdoches, Texas 75964
TELEPHONE:	(936) 559-1125
E-MAIL:	reservations@fairbreezecabin.com
WEBSITE:	www.fairbreezecabin.com
ROOMS:	1 Cabin; Private bath
CHILDREN:	Children age 12 and older welcome
ANIMALS:	Not allowed
HANDICAPPED:	Not handicapped accessible
DIETARY NEEDS:	Will accommodate guests' special dietary needs

Bacon Spinach Quiche

Serves 6

Serve with fruit for breakfast or with a green salad for lunch or dinner. This recipe can easily be doubled for larger groups.

8	ounces bacon
1	(9-inch) regular-size pie shell (thawed or homemade)
6	eggs
½	cup sour cream (light or regular)
½	(10-ounce) package frozen chopped spinach, cooked and drained well
1	cup (4 ounces) grated colby/Jack cheese (light or regular)

Salt and pepper, to taste

Cook bacon until crisp. Drain on paper towels (reserve a little of the bacon grease and brush it onto the bottom of the pie shell – this adds a lot of flavor). Crumble the bacon into the pie shell.

Preheat oven to 350°F. Beat eggs and sour cream together in a large bowl. Pour the egg mixture over the bacon in the pie shell. Spread the spinach over the egg mixture. Spread the cheese over the spinach. Season with salt and pepper. Bake for 45 minutes, or until the top of the quiche is golden brown. Cool for 10 minutes before slicing and serving.

Angelsgate

The Angelsgate Bed & Breakfast is a National Historic Landmark nestled in historic Bryan. This lovely historic home was built in 1909. The Houston architectural firm Jones & Tabor designed the house in a style often referred to as the "American Foursquare."

The inn is within a 10-minute drive of Texas A&M University and the George Bush Presidential Library. Messina Hof Winery is also located nearby. Guests may also enjoy browsing the antique shops in Bryan.

INNKEEPERS:	Nita Harding
ADDRESS:	615 East 29th Street
	Bryan, Texas 77803
TELEPHONE:	(979) 779-1231; (888) 779-1231
E-MAIL:	stay@angelsgate.com
WEBSITE:	www.angelsgate.com
ROOMS:	1 Room; 2 Suites; Private baths
CHILDREN:	Children age 13 and older welcome
ANIMALS:	Not allowed
HANDICAPPED:	Not handicapped accessible
DIETARY NEEDS:	Will accommodate guests' special dietary needs

Picante Quiche

Makes 6 Servings

1   cup picante sauce (hot or mild)
1   cup (4 ounces) grated Monterey Jack cheese
1   cup (4 ounces) grated cheddar cheese
6   eggs
¾   cup sour cream
1   tablespoon chopped fresh chives
⅛   teaspoon garlic powder
½   cup (2 ounces) grated fresh Parmesan cheese
Paprika
Chopped fresh parsley or cilantro

Preheat oven to 350°F. Spray a 9- or 10-inch pie pan with nonstick cooking spray. Spread picante sauce over the bottom of the pie pan. Layer with the Monterey Jack and cheddar cheeses. Combine eggs, sour cream, chives and garlic powder; pour over the cheese layers. Top with Parmesan cheese and sprinkle with paprika and parsley or cilantro.

Bake for 40 minutes. Let stand for 10 minutes before serving.

Rosevine Inn

Located in Tyler, "The Rose Capital of the World," the Rosevine Inn Bed & Breakfast is situated on one of Tyler's quaint brick streets near the Azalea District. Although the original house burned down, the Rosevine Inn was constructed in 1986 to replicate a 1930's-style home, while being designed to accommodate the needs of modern travelers.

The Sherlock Holmes Suite is, of course, decorated in Old English style. (If you are a sleuth, perhaps you will find the hidden door to receive a gift!)

INNKEEPERS:	Rebecca & Bert Powell
ADDRESS:	415 South Vine
	Tyler, Texas 75702
TELEPHONE:	(903) 592-2221
EMAIL:	rosevine@iamerica.net
WEBSITE:	www.rosevine.com
ROOMS:	6 Rooms; 1 Suite; 2 Cottages; Private baths
CHILDREN:	Children age 5 and older welcome
ANIMALS:	Not allowed; Resident outdoor cats
HANDICAPPED:	Not handicapped accessible
DIETARY NEEDS:	Will accommodate guests' special dietary needs

Sunshine Quiche

Makes 6 to 8 Servings

1	pound breakfast sausage
⅓	cup finely chopped onion
1	cup (4 ounces) grated cheese (cheddar, Swiss, mozzarella or a mixture)
2	cups milk
4	eggs
1	cup baking mix (such as Bisquick)
¼	teaspoon salt
⅛	teaspoon pepper

Preheat oven to 400°F. Spray a 10-inch quiche or pie pan with nonstick cooking spray. Cook sausage and onion in a large skillet over medium-low heat until sausage is cooked through and onions are soft; drain any grease. Put sausage mixture in the pan. Sprinkle with cheese.

Beat together milk and eggs in a large bowl. Add baking mix, salt and pepper. Mix until well blended and smooth. Pour egg mixture over sausage and cheese. Bake for 35 minutes, or until set. Let stand for 5 minutes. Cut into wedges and serve.

Old Mulberry Inn

B uilt in the style of a northern Louisiana plantation, the Old Mulberry Inn Bed & Breakfast is a stunning combination of 21st-century comforts and 19th-century charm. The owners chose an architectural style that represents the antebellum heyday of Jefferson, culling antique shops and salvage yards to furnish the stately Greek Revival inn.

Located in the historic district, the inn offers five distinctively decorated guest rooms and three-course gourmet breakfasts.

INNKEEPERS:	Donald & Gloria Degn
ADDRESS:	209 Jefferson Street
	Jefferson, Texas 75657
TELEPHONE:	(903) 665-1945; (800) 263-5319
E-MAIL:	mulberry@jeffersontx.com
WEBSITE:	www.oldmulberryinn.com
ROOMS:	5 Rooms; Private baths
CHILDREN:	Children age 15 and older welcome
ANIMALS:	Not allowed
HANDICAPPED:	Not handicapped accessible
DIETARY NEEDS:	Will accommodate guests' special dietary needs

Red & Green Pepper Quiche

Makes 6 to 8 Servings

5	eggs
1	(12-ounce) carton small-curd cottage cheese
¼	cup flour
½	teaspoon baking powder
2	tablespoons butter, melted plus 1 tablespoon butter
2	cups (8 ounces) grated Monterey Jack or pepper Jack cheese, divided
1	small yellow onion, chopped
½	green bell pepper, chopped
½	red bell pepper, chopped
4	green onions, chopped (optional)

Preheat oven to 350°F. Spray a 10-inch pie or quiche pan with nonstick cooking spray. In a large bowl, whisk together eggs, cottage cheese, flour, baking powder, 2 tablespoons melted butter and 1 cup grated cheese.

Melt 1 tablespoon of butter in a small skillet over medium-low heat. Add the onion; cook until onions are tender and just slightly browned. Stir the onions into the egg mixture. Add green and red bell pepper and green onions; stir to mix well. Pour the mixture into the pan. Sprinkle with the remaining 1 cup of grated cheese. Bake for about 35 minutes, or until lightly browned. Let stand for 5-10 minutes before serving.

Karbach Haus

The Karbach Haus is a historic mansion that maintains the character of generations past, graciously blended with the modern amenities of a small, upscale resort. Six spacious bedrooms have private tile baths, some with Jacuzzis. A swimming pool and spa are set among stately old trees in beautifully landscaped gardens.

Located on a one-acre estate near the city center, guests are a short stroll from a superb variety of restaurants, museums and antique stores.

INNKEEPERS:	Kathy & Ben Jack Kinney
ADDRESS:	487 West San Antonio Street
	New Braunfels, Texas 78130
TELEPHONE:	(830) 625-2131; (800) 972-5941
E-MAIL:	khausbnb@aol.com
WEBSITE:	www.karbachhaus.com
ROOMS:	4 Rooms; 2 Suites; Private baths
CHILDREN:	Not allowed
ANIMALS:	Not allowed
HANDICAPPED:	Not handicapped accessible
DIETARY NEEDS:	Will accommodate guests' special dietary needs

Mushroom, Spinach, Onion & Cheese Pie

Serves 6 to 8

1 tablespoon butter
1 (8-ounce) package sliced fresh mushrooms
1 bunch green onions, chopped
1 tablespoon diced pimento
2 cups fresh baby spinach leaves, washed and dried (or use bagged, ready-to-eat)
2 cups (8 ounces) grated colby/Jack cheese (or cheese of choice)
3 eggs
¾ cup baking mix (such as Bisquick) (use regular, not buttermilk mix)
2 cups 2% or whole milk
¼ teaspoon salt

Preheat oven to 350°F. Spray a 10-inch deep-dish pie pan with nonstick cooking spray. Melt butter in a skillet over medium-low heat. Add mushrooms and onions; cook until tender and all of the excess liquid from the mushrooms has evaporated. Stir in the diced pimento.

Line the bottom of the pie pan with spinach leaves. Top with mushroom mixture. Sprinkle cheese on top.

Beat eggs, baking mix, milk and salt together (some lumps will still be visible). Pour over the ingredients in the pie pan. Bake for 45 minutes, or until puffed and golden on top (if the pie starts to get too brown, cover with foil during the last 15 minutes of baking). Let stand for 10 minutes before slicing.

Note: This recipe is easily doubled. Use a 9x13-inch baking dish and bake for 1 hour.

Munzesheimer Manor

Munzesheimer Manor is a magnificent testimony to the Victorian era, built at the turn of the century by a German immigrant for his new bride. The house features large rooms with high ceilings, seven fireplaces with antique mantles, many bay windows and a large wrap-around porch complete with rocking chairs and wicker furniture.

"One of the 12 best bed and breakfasts in Texas." ~ *The Dallas Morning News*

INNKEEPERS:	Bob & Sherry Murray
ADDRESS:	202 North Newsom
	Mineola, Texas 75773
TELEPHONE:	(903) 569-6634
E-MAIL:	innkeeper@munzesheimer.com
WEBSITE:	www.munzesheimer.com
ROOMS:	4 Rooms; 3 Cottages; Private baths
CHILDREN:	Welcome; Call ahead
ANIMALS:	Not allowed; Resident dog
HANDICAPPED:	Call ahead
DIETARY NEEDS:	Will accommodate guests' special dietary needs

Chile Cheese Puff

Makes 8 Servings

"This is a 'real' Texas breakfast served with biscuits and gravy and lots of hot coffee." ~ Innkeeper, Munzesheimer Manor

2   (4-ounce) cans chopped green chiles, drained
4   cups (16 ounces) grated cheddar/Jack cheese
14 large eggs
2   cups milk
¼   cup baking mix (such as Bisquick)
Salsa, for serving
Sour cream, for serving

Preheat oven to 350°F. Spread chiles in an ungreased 9x13-inch baking dish. Cover chiles with cheese. Whisk together eggs, milk and baking mix in a large bowl; pour over cheese. Bake for 40-45 minutes. Cut into squares and serve with salsa and sour cream.

Austin's Wildflower Inn

Throughout Austin's Wildflower Inn you will see the beautiful, original oak hardwood floors, antique furniture in every room, hand-made quilts and elegant lace curtains. A spacious porch graces the front of the house with comfortable chairs for enjoying the beautiful front gardens.

A shaded stone patio under the beautiful Texas oak tree in the side yard is a great way to pass the afternoon sipping iced tea.

INNKEEPERS:	Kay Jackson & Claudean Schultz
ADDRESS:	1200 West 22½ Street
	Austin, Texas 78705
TELEPHONE:	(512) 477-9639
E-MAIL:	kjackson@austinswildflowerinn.com
WEBSITE:	www.austinswildflowerinn.com
ROOMS:	3 Rooms; Private baths
CHILDREN:	Call ahead
ANIMALS:	Not allowed
HANDICAPPED:	Not handicapped accessible
DIETARY NEEDS:	Call ahead

Wildflower Garden Loaf

Makes 6 to 8 Servings

1	loaf (1-pound) ciabatta bread (a wide, thin-crusted Italian bread)
8	tablespoons butter, divided
1½	teaspoons plus 1 teaspoon garlic powder, or more to taste
½	cup chopped onion
1	cup sliced mushrooms
1	cup grated zucchini
1	cup grated carrot

Salt and pepper

6	eggs
¾	cup whole milk
3	tablespoons (1½ ounces) cream cheese
½	teaspoon chopped dill, or to taste
2	cups (8 ounces) grated cheese (colby/longhorn/Jack mixture is good)
1	tomato, sliced ¼-inch thick

Preheat oven to 350°F. Cut off the top of the bread; reserve the top. Pull out the soft center of the bread, leaving just enough around the edges and bottom to make a "bowl." Melt 5 tablespoons butter; stir in 1½ teaspoons garlic powder to make garlic-butter. Brush bottom and sides of bread bowl and bottom of reserved bread top with 3-4 tablespoons of garlic-butter (reserve 1-2 tablespoons). Melt 2 tablespoons butter in a large skillet over medium heat. Cook onions, mushrooms, zucchini and carrots until crisp-tender. Season with salt and pepper (about ½ teaspoon each) and 1 teaspoon garlic powder, or more to taste. (Note: the garlic really makes a difference.)

Beat eggs and milk. Season with salt and pepper. Melt the remaining 1 tablespoon of butter in a skillet over medium heat; add the egg mixture. Add the cream cheese, pinching it off into bits. Add the dill. Stir gently, but constantly, until cream cheese has melted and eggs are set (eggs should be moist and fluffy, but not too wet). Put bread bowl on a lightly greased baking sheet. Sprinkle 1 cup of cheese into it. Spoon cooked egg mixture over cheese. Spoon vegetable mixture over eggs. Cover with tomato slices. Top with remaining cheese. Cover with bread top. Cover the top loosely with foil. Bake for 25-30 minutes, or until heated through. Remove loaf from oven. Brush top and sides with the remaining garlic-butter. Slice and serve.

Side Dishes

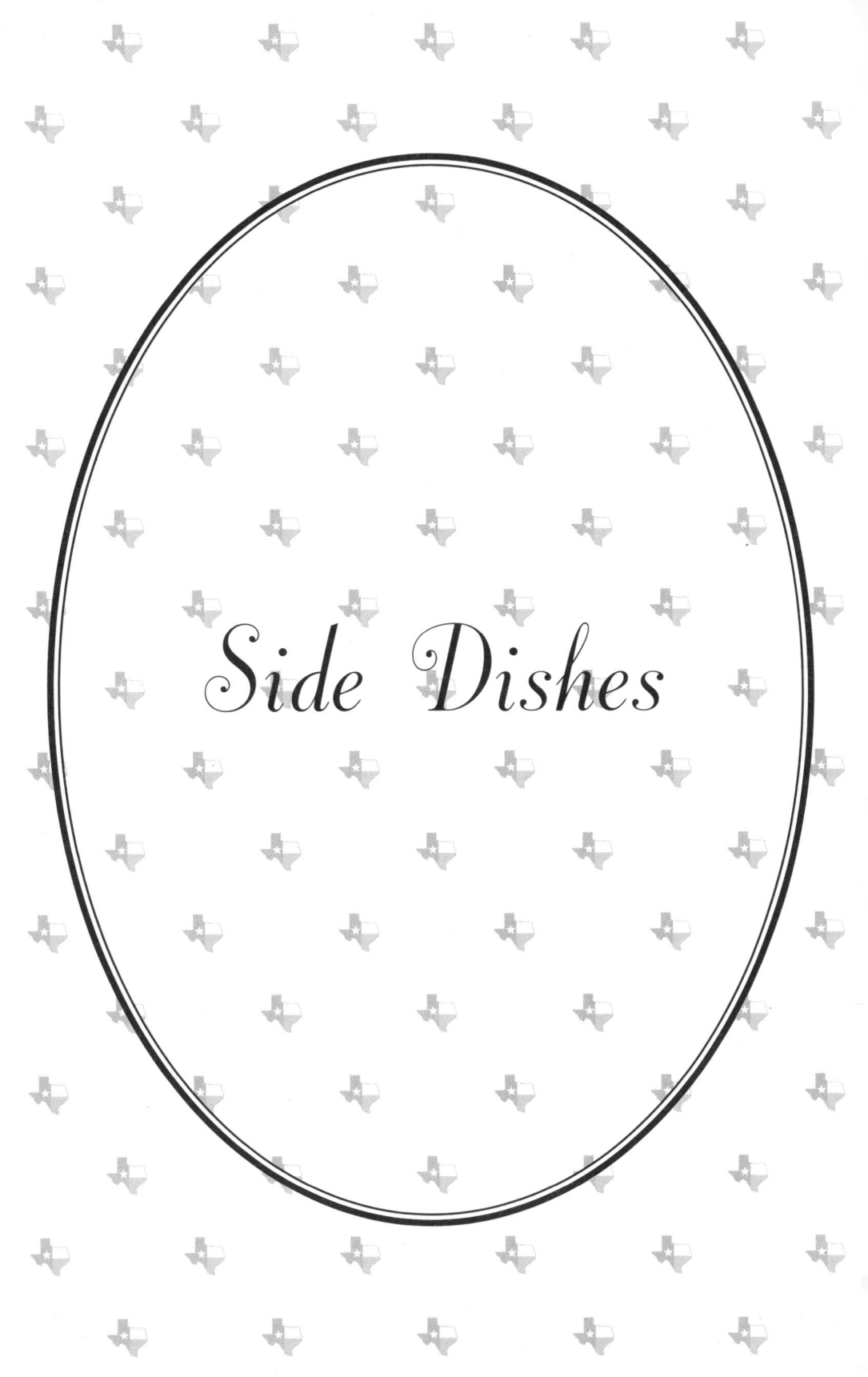

Side Dishes

Christmas House

Built in 1908, the Christmas House Bed & Breakfast is located in San Antonio's Monte Vista Historic District, where guests find a warm and festive atmosphere year-round. The house is filled with beautiful ornaments, angels, holiday collectibles, antiques, handmade quilts and much more.

If you see an ornament or collectable at the Christmas House that you just cannot live without, most of the antiques and furnishings are available for purchase.

INNKEEPERS:	Penny & Grant Estes
ADDRESS:	2307 McCullough
	San Antonio, Texas 78212
TELEPHONE:	(210) 737-2786; (800) 268-4187
E-MAIL:	christmashsb@earthlink.net
WEBSITE:	www.christmashousebnb.com
ROOMS:	4 Rooms; 1 Suite; Private baths
CHILDREN:	Welcome
ANIMALS:	Not allowed; Resident cat
HANDICAPPED:	Handicapped accessible
DIETARY NEEDS:	Will accommodate guests' special dietary needs

Christmas House Potato Casserole

Makes 8 to 10 Servings

Other ingredients (turkey, chicken, chopped black olives, etc.) can be added or substituted, depending on your taste or what you have on hand.

2	cups sour cream
1	(30-ounce) package frozen hash browns (no need to thaw)
2	(10¾-ounce) cans cream of mushroom or potato soup
1	medium onion, chopped
2	cups (8 ounces) grated cheddar cheese
1	cup (about) cubed cooked ham
1	green bell pepper, chopped
1	(8-ounce) can sliced mushrooms
1	(2.8-ounce) can French fried onions

Preheat oven to 350°F. Spray a 9x13-inch baking dish with nonstick cooking spray. Combine all ingredients, except the French fried onions, in a very large bowl; pour into the dish. Cover with foil and bake for 1 hour.

Remove from oven, remove foil and gently stir. Bake, uncovered, for 25 minutes more. Remove from oven again and sprinkle French fried onions over the casserole. Bake for 5 minutes more, or until onions are golden.

Note: This casserole may be assembled ahead, except for the French fried onions, and refrigerated or frozen. If frozen, let thaw in the refrigerator overnight before baking.

George Blucher House

Breakfast at the George Blucher House is quite an affair. Guests have compared it to an elegant dinner party. Served by candlelight in the inn's beautiful dining room, often on the innkeeper's great-grandmother's china, with sterling silver flatware, crystal stemware and exquisite linens, the inn's breakfasts are multi-course gourmet delights.

During late fall and early spring, breakfast may be served outdoors on the back veranda where guests dine bistro-style on white, French wrought iron tables and chairs overlooking the koi pond with fountain.

INNKEEPERS:	Tracey Love Smith
ADDRESS:	211 North Carrizo
	Corpus Christi, Texas 78401
TELEPHONE:	(361) 884-4884; (866) 884-4884
E-MAIL:	innkeeper@georgeblucherhouse.com
WEBSITE:	www. georgeblucherhouse.com
ROOMS:	5 Rooms; 1 Suite; Private baths
CHILDREN:	Call ahead
ANIMALS:	Not allowed; Resident dog & cat
HANDICAPPED:	Call ahead
DIETARY NEEDS:	Will accommodate guests' special dietary needs

Hash Brown Casserole

Makes 10 Servings

1   (30-ounce) bag frozen shredded hash brown potatoes
1   small yellow onion, chopped
1   stick (½ cup) butter, melted
8   ounces Velveeta cheese, melted
1   cup sour cream
1   (10-ounce) can cream of chicken soup

Topping:
1½ cups crushed corn flakes
½   stick (¼ cup) butter, melted

Preheat oven to 325°F. Put frozen potatoes and chopped onions in an ungreased 9x13-inch baking dish. Pour 1 stick of melted butter over the potatoes and onions. Combine melted Velveeta, sour cream and soup; pour over the ingredients in the baking dish.

Top with crushed corn flakes. Drizzle ½ stick of melted butter over the corn flakes. Bake, uncovered, for 45-60 minutes (the longer it bakes, the crisper the top).

Note: This dish can be prepared a day ahead (except for the corn flakes and the ½ stick melted butter topping), covered and refrigerated. Top with the corn flakes and ½ stick of melted butter just before baking.

Christmas House

The Christmas House Bed & Breakfast is located in San Antonio, near the Alamo and the River Walk. Guests are invited to come enjoy the city that boasts of beautiful views, historic architecture, a bustling riverfront and carefully manicured parks.

The Santa Claus Room is decorated with red and white accents and is furnished with an 1880, inlaid rosewood queen-size bed with an armoire and a private veranda.

INNKEEPERS:	Penny & Grant Estes
ADDRESS:	2307 McCullough
	San Antonio, Texas 78212
TELEPHONE:	(210) 737-2786; (800) 268-4187
E-MAIL:	christmashsb@earthlink.net
WEBSITE:	www.christmashousebnb.com
ROOMS:	4 Rooms; 1 Suite; Private baths
CHILDREN:	Welcome
ANIMALS:	Not allowed; Resident cat
HANDICAPPED:	Handicapped accessible
DIETARY NEEDS:	Will accommodate guests' special dietary needs

Christmas House
Hash Brown Bake

Makes 4 to 6 Servings

"This dish may be assembled the night before, omitting the egg mixture. In the morning, let the dish stand at room temperature for 30 minutes, then add the egg mixture and bake as directed. Other ingredients can be added or substituted, such as chicken, turkey, sausage, pimentos, etc. Leftovers are great for dinner!" ~ Innkeeper, Christmas House Bed & Breakfast

3   cups frozen shredded potatoes, thawed
1   stick (½ cup) butter, melted
1   cup finely chopped cooked ham
1   cup (4 ounces) grated cheese of choice
¼   cup finely chopped green bell pepper
1   (6-ounce) can mushroom pieces
Chopped onion, to taste
2   large eggs, beaten
½   cup milk
½   teaspoon salt
¼   teaspoon pepper

Preheat oven to 425°F. Put thawed potatoes between paper towels; press to remove excess moisture. Spread potatoes into an ungreased 9-inch pie pan, pressing them onto the bottom and up the sides of the pan to form a shell. Drizzle melted butter evenly over the potatoes. Bake for 25 minutes, or until slightly browned. Cool on a wire rack.

Lower oven temperature to 350°F. Combine ham, cheese, green pepper, mushrooms and onions. Spoon mixture into the cooled potato shell. Combine eggs, milk, salt and pepper in a small bowl; beat well using a fork or a whisk. Pour over the ingredients in the pan. Bake for 25-30 minutes, or until set. Let stand for 10 minutes before serving.

The English Manor

Shortly after the English Manor was built, the homeowner decided to add a kitchen that could accommodate the whole town for Sunday breakfast. With that sort of kitchen, imagine what a treat breakfast is today! Breakfasts include coffee cakes, delicious egg entrées and homemade jams.

The Raffles Cargo Hold Room features a unique collection of Asian, African and Indian treasures. Enjoy an evening under a canopy bed in the tradition of such adventurers as Sir Richard Burton and Jim Thompson.

INNKEEPERS:	Lynette Sarnoski
ADDRESS:	540 El Paso Street
	Jacksonville, Texas 75766
TELEPHONE:	(903) 541-4694; (800) 866-0946
E-MAIL:	lsarnoski@hotmail.com
WEBSITE:	www.englishmanorbedandbreakfast.com
ROOMS:	7 Rooms; Private baths
CHILDREN:	Welcome
ANIMALS:	Welcome in 1 room; Resident parrots
HANDICAPPED:	Handicapped accessible
DIETARY NEEDS:	Call ahead

Sweet Potato Soufflé

Makes 8 to 10 Servings

"Absolutely delicious — even children love it. This soufflé is great with smoked meats." - Innkeeper, The English Manor

3	cups (about) mashed sweet potatoes (or drained, mashed canned)
½	stick (¼ cup) butter, room temperature
1	cup sugar
½	cup evaporated milk
2	eggs
½	teaspoon nutmeg
½	teaspoon cinnamon
1	teaspoon vanilla extract
1	teaspoon imitation butter flavoring (optional)

Topping:

½	cup crushed Frosted Flakes
½	cup nuts
½	cup packed light brown sugar
½	stick (¼ cup) butter, room temperature

Preheat oven to 350°F. Spray a 9x13-inch baking dish with nonstick cooking spray. Combine sweet potatoes, butter, sugar, milk, eggs, nutmeg, cinnamon, vanilla and butter flavoring. Spread in the baking dish.

Combine all of the topping ingredients in a medium bowl with a fork. Sprinkle evenly over potato mixture. Bake for 45-50 minutes, or until heated through.

The Inn at Craig Place

The Inn at Craig Place Bed & Breakfast welcomes you to the exciting, colorful and historic city of San Antonio. This stately home was built in 1891, and is listed on the National Historic Registry as part of the historic Monte Vista neighborhood. Wrap-around twin porches invite you to enter the lovely house where you can relax in pampered contentment.

In the morning, the aroma of brewing coffee and the fragrance of fresh baked goods beckon you from your nest of feather pillows and down blankets.

INNKEEPERS:	Tamra, Sandy & John Black
ADDRESS:	117 West Craig Place
	San Antonio, Texas 78212
TELEPHONE:	(210) 736-1017; (877) 427-2447
E-MAIL:	stay@craigplace.com
WEBSITE:	www.craigplace.com
ROOMS:	3 Rooms; 1 Suite; Private baths
CHILDREN:	Children age 12 and older welcome
ANIMALS:	Not allowed; Resident cat
HANDICAPPED:	Not handicapped accessible
DIETARY NEEDS:	Will accommodate guests' special dietary needs

Sweet Potato Salad

Makes 8 Servings

This delicious, unusual warm salad takes only minutes to put together if some of the preparation is done in advance. Try cooking the bacon and sweet potatoes ahead of time, as well as chopping the scallions and toasting the pecans – you'll be a relaxed host or hostess when serving.

1   (12-ounce) package bacon
½   bunch scallions (green onions), chopped
¼   cup apple cider vinegar
⅓   cup maple syrup, or more to taste
¼   cup dried cranberries or Craisins
2   pounds sweet potatoes, peeled, cubed and cooked (about 3 cups)
½   bunch parsley, chopped (more or less, to taste)
½   cup toasted pecans

Cook and crumble the bacon (reserve 1 tablespoon of bacon grease). Heat the reserved 1 tablespoon of bacon grease in a large skillet. Add scallions and cook for 2 minutes, or until soft. Deglaze pan with vinegar and cook until liquid is reduced by half. Add maple syrup; cook for 2 minutes more. Stir in dried cranberries and bacon. Add cubed sweet potatoes and parsley; stir to combine. Serve warm or at room temperature. Garnish with toasted pecans just before serving.

Ragtime Ranch Inn

G uests entering the gate to the Ragtime Ranch Inn immediately feel the ranch's country grace, with green pastures on one side and thick woods on the other. The inn offers a quiet Texas getaway with traditional ranch-style porches, stocked fishing pond, stable, 37 acres of nature trails and a cool, shaded swimming pool.

Bird watchers can keep an eye out for the many species of birds who call Ragtime Ranch Inn home.

INNKEEPERS:	Roberta Butler & Debbie Jameson
ADDRESS:	203 Ragtime Ranch Road
	Elgin, Texas 78621
TELEPHONE:	(512) 285-9599; (800) 800-9743
E-MAIL:	ragtimeinn@earthlink.net
WEBSITE:	www.ragtimeinn.com
ROOMS:	4 Rooms; Private baths
CHILDREN:	Welcome
ANIMALS:	Welcome (even horses!); Resident dogs & cats
HANDICAPPED:	Call ahead
DIETARY NEEDS:	Will accommodate guests' special dietary needs

Cowpoke Beans

Makes 12 Servings

"These beans won first prize in the vegetable division at the 1997 Elgin Western Days Food Fair. To make vegetarian Cowpoke Beans, substitute 4 tablespoons olive oil for the bacon and bacon drippings." ~ Innkeeper, Ragtime Ranch Inn

2   tablespoons bacon drippings
4   thick, lean slices uncooked bacon, chopped
2   cups chopped onion
1   large clove garlic, minced
2   (14½-ounce) cans stewed tomatoes, undrained
¼   cup chopped fresh parsley
½   teaspoon cumin
½   teaspoon marjoram
5   teaspoons chili powder
Salt, to taste
4   (15-ounce) cans Ranch style beans, rinsed and drained
Water or beer (enough to cover beans)

Heat bacon drippings in a large saucepot over medium heat. Add bacon, onion and garlic; cook until onion is tender. Add tomatoes, parsley, cumin, marjoram, chili powder and salt. Bring to a boil, lower the heat and simmer gently for 45 minutes.

Add the beans. Pour in enough water or beer to cover the beans. Simmer for 20 minutes more.

The Texas White House

Families staying at the Texas White House Bed & Breakfast will love the nearby zoo, the Log Cabin Village, Trinity Park, the Omni Theater and the Water Gardens. Romantic couples will find fine restaurants, privacy and relaxation. The inn boasts Jacuzzi tubs, a sauna, luxurious beds and a breakfast "fit for visiting royalty."

The Land of Contrast Room features a sitting area, wicker furniture and a Texas king-size bath with claw-foot tub and shower.

INNKEEPERS:	Jamie & Grover McMains
ADDRESS:	1417 Eighth Avenue
	Fort Worth, Texas 76104
TELEPHONE:	(817) 923-3597; (800) 279-6491
E-MAIL:	txwhitehou@aol.com
WEBSITE:	www.texaswhitehouse.com
ROOMS:	3 Rooms; 2 Suites; Private baths
CHILDREN:	Welcome
ANIMALS:	Call ahead
HANDICAPPED:	Handicapped accessible
DIETARY NEEDS:	Will accommodate guests' special dietary needs

Green Bean Bundles

Makes 4 to 6 Servings

Great as a side dish for pot roast or baked turkey.

2   (14½-ounce) cans whole green beans, drained
6   slices uncooked bacon, each slice cut into fourths
⅓   cup packed brown sugar
1   stick (½ cup) butter
⅛   teaspoon minced garlic

Preheat oven to 350°F. Wrap 4 or 5 beans in ¼ slice of bacon, making 24 bundles (there is no need for toothpicks – the bacon sticks to itself.) Arrange bundles in an ungreased 7x11-inch baking pan.

Put brown sugar, butter and garlic in a saucepan; bring to a boil and stir until well mixed. Pour over the green bean bundles.

Bake, uncovered, for 20 minutes. Cover the pan with foil and bake for 30 minutes more. Serve 4-6 bundles per person.

Sierra Diablo Ranch & Lodge

The Sierra Diablo Ranch & Lodge is a working cattle ranch. There is always plenty to do for those who want to get their hands dirty. The innkeepers also want guests to relax, put their feet up and enjoy some southwest Texas hospitality. You can hang around the homestead where the coffee pot is always on the fire, or saddle up and ride the range.

The Sierra Diablo is the home of Victorio Canyon where the last Apache Indian battle in Texas was fought.

INNKEEPERS:	Woodrow & Sandra Bean
ADDRESS:	2.8 Miles Northeast of Sierra Blanca
	Sierra Blanca, Texas 79851
TELEPHONE:	(915) 986-2502; (800) 986-9940
E-MAIL:	ranch@sierradiablo.com
WEBSITE:	www.sierradiablo.com
ROOMS:	5 Rooms; 1 Suite; Private & shared baths
CHILDREN:	Children age 16 and older welcome
ANIMALS:	Not allowed
HANDICAPPED:	Not handicapped accessible
DIETARY NEEDS:	Will accommodate guests' special dietary needs

Spanish Squash Casserole

Makes 12 Servings

Even if squash isn't your favorite vegetable, you'll love this casserole! Using a mixture of zucchini and yellow squash creates a very colorful dish.

8   medium zucchini, yellow squash or a mixture, cut into ½-inch
    pieces
1   medium onion, chopped
Salt and pepper, to taste
1   (4-ounce) can chopped green chilies
1   (14½-ounce) can diced tomatoes, drained
2   eggs, beaten
1   cup dry bread crumbs
1   cup (4 ounces) grated cheddar cheese

Put zucchini and onion in a large saucepan. Cover with water. Bring to a boil, lower heat and simmer until tender, 12-15 minutes. Drain.

Preheat oven to 350°F. Put zucchini mixture in a large bowl and mash. Season with salt and pepper. Add green chilies, tomatoes, eggs and bread crumbs; mix well. Pour the mixture into a greased 9x13-inch baking dish. Sprinkle grated cheese on top. Bake, uncovered, for 30 minutes.

The English Manor

T he English Manor is located in an English Tudor house, built in 1932 by lumber baron Willie Brown. Uniquely different, the English Manor offers a lovely, private garden and six distinctive theme rooms with eclectic furnishings, designer linens, feather beds and large private baths.

Located in the beautiful Texas Piney Woods, the inn is just minutes from Lake Jacksonville, numerous antique malls, the rustic Palestine Railway and the beautiful Tyler Rose Gardens.

INNKEEPERS:	Lynette Sarnoski
ADDRESS:	540 El Paso Street
	Jacksonville, Texas 75766
TELEPHONE:	(903) 541-4694; (800) 866-0946
E-MAIL:	lsarnoski@hotmail.com
WEBSITE:	www.englishmanorbedandbreakfast.com
ROOMS:	7 Rooms; Private baths
CHILDREN:	Welcome
ANIMALS:	Welcome in 1 room; Resident parrots
HANDICAPPED:	Handicapped accessible
DIETARY NEEDS:	Call ahead

Mushroom Bake

Makes 6 to 8 Servings

"This mushroom dish can be used as a tasty substitute for potatoes with either beef or chicken. It is also a nice accompaniment for egg dishes." ~ Innkeeper, The English Manor

½	cup mayonnaise
6	slices bread
1	tablespoon butter
½	cup chopped onion
½	cup sliced celery
1	pound fresh mushrooms, sliced
½	cup chopped green bell pepper
1	(10½-ounce) can cream of mushroom soup
2	eggs
¾	teaspoon salt
¼	teaspoon pepper
1	cup (about) croutons

Preheat oven to 325°F. Spray a 2½-quart casserole dish with nonstick cooking spray (an 8x10½-inch oval or an 8½-inch round casserole dish works well).

Spread mayonnaise on 1 side of each bread slice. Cut the bread slices into ½-inch cubes; set aside. Melt butter in a large skillet. Add onion, celery, mushrooms and green pepper; cook until tender. Drain any liquid.

Put ½ of the bread cubes in the casserole dish. Top with the mushroom mixture, then the remaining bread cubes. In a medium bowl, combine soup, eggs, salt and pepper; pour over the ingredients in the casserole dish. Sprinkle croutons on top. Bake, uncovered, for 1 hour.

The Cook's Cottage & Suites

The Cook's Cottage & Suites' innkeeper, Patsy Bynum Swendson, is a nationally recognized authority on Southwestern cuisine who has delighted radio and television audiences for over 20 years, authored 49 cookbooks and been a contributing writer for nine national magazines.

Located in the heart of the Texas Hill Country, The Cook's Cottage has been selected by *Travel and Leisure* magazine as "One of the Top 25 Most Romantic Places in the U.S."

INNKEEPERS:	Patsy Swendson
ADDRESS:	703 West Austin
	Fredericksburg, Texas 78624
TELEPHONE:	(210) 493-5101; (210) 273-6471
E-MAIL:	patsy@aisi.net
WEBSITE:	www.bed-inn-breakfast-tx.com
ROOMS:	3 Rooms; 2 Suites; 1 Cottage; Private baths
CHILDREN:	Not allowed
ANIMALS:	Not allowed
HANDICAPPED:	Not handicapped accessible
DIETARY NEEDS:	Will accommodate guests' special dietary needs

Melon with Black Forest Ham & Strawberry Salsa

Makes 4 Servings

"Slices of cool, fragrant cantaloupe topped with thin slices of Black Forest ham is yummy enough, but paired with ginger- and orange-scented strawberry salsa, you can't help but win! A wonderful side dish for brunch." - Innkeeper, The Cook's Cottage & Suites

1   **large ripe cantaloupe**
6   **ounces Black Forest ham, sliced into thin julienne strips**
Strawberry salsa (recipe follows)

Cut cantaloupe in half and remove seeds. Cut melon halves into thick slices. Chill until ready to serve.

Arrange the melon on a serving plate. Sprinkle strips of ham over the melon. Serve with strawberry salsa.

Strawberry salsa:
8   **ounces strawberries, hulled and diced**
1   **teaspoon sugar**
2   **tablespoons freshly squeezed orange juice**
1   **teaspoon grated orange zest**
½   **teaspoon finely grated fresh ginger**

Combine diced berries and sugar; crush berries slightly to release juices. Stir in orange juice, orange zest and ginger.

Bonita - A Stagecoach Stop

Stagecoach Stop B+B

Bonita - A Stagecoach Stop is just five miles from Gruene, between New Braunfels and San Marcos. The inn is truly a visit to the past. It was used as a stagecoach stop until 1868 and was an Amish homestead before being turned into an inn for modern travelers.

You'll discover another era as you pass through the doors of the Log Pen Cabin, which was constructed in 1848, and the German Fachwerk house, which was built in 1850.

INNKEEPERS:	Bettina & Jeff Messinger
ADDRESS:	5441 FM 1102
	New Braunfels, Texas 78132
TELEPHONE:	(830) 620-9453
E-MAIL:	stagecoach@satx.rr.com
WEBSITE:	www.stagecoachbedandbreakfast.com
ROOMS:	4 Rooms; 1 Suite; 4 Cottages; Private baths
CHILDREN:	Welcome
ANIMALS:	Not allowed; Resident dog, cat & rabbits
HANDICAPPED:	Handicapped accessible
DIETARY NEEDS:	Will accommodate guests' special dietary needs

Pink Grapefruit Apple Dish

Makes 6 Servings

A very refreshing taste. This is a great side dish with sausage and eggs.

3   pink grapefruit (or use the ready-to-eat grapefruit in a jar)
3   sweet, firm apples, peeled, cored and thinly sliced
Fresh chopped mint, to taste

Peel and section the grapefruit, placing the pieces in a large bowl. Add apple slices to the grapefruit; toss to coat the apples with grapefruit juice. Chill. Before serving, add fresh mint. This is very colorful served in individual clear glass dishes.

Luncheon & Dinner Entrées

Luncheon & Dinner Entrées

Blair House

B lair House is a fine country inn that offers something for everyone. Whether you are looking for rest and relaxation, a stimulating writers' retreat or a cooking class, look no further! The food at this inn is magnificent. Chef Christopher Stonesifer recently won second prize in the annual Taste of San Antonio culinary competition.

"A five-star dining experience ... the place to stay in Wimberley." ~
D Magazine

INNKEEPERS:	Mike & Vickie Schneider
ADDRESS:	100 Spoke Hill Road
	Wimberley, Texas 78676
TELEPHONE:	(512) 847-1111; (877) 549-5450
E-MAIL:	info@blairhouseinn.com
WEBSITE:	www.blairhouseinn.com
ROOMS:	9 Rooms; Private baths
CHILDREN:	Children age 12 and older welcome
ANIMALS:	Not allowed; Resident dog
HANDICAPPED:	Handicapped accessible
DIETARY NEEDS:	Will accommodate guests' special dietary needs

Chef Christopher's Brisk
East-Texas Style

Makes 8 to 10

5   quarts (20 cups) good beef stock
2   cups dry red wine
2   bay leaves
1   tablespoon whole black peppercorns
3   cloves garlic, lightly crushed
¼   cup kosher or sea salt
1   (4- to 5-pound) beef brisket, fat cap on
1¼   cups favorite barbecue sauce, plus additional for serving.

In a large stockpot, combine beef stock, wine, bay leaves, peppercorns, garlic and salt. Bring the mixture to a low boil. Place the brisket in the boiling liquid and cook at a low simmer until tender, about 1½ hours.

Remove the meat from the liquid and place on the top rack of a grill or smoker. Smoke for 60 minutes, basting with barbecue sauce. Let brisket rest on a cutting board for 15 minutes. Trim excess fat and slice the brisket very thinly across the grain. Serve with additional barbecue sauce, if desired.

Sierra Diablo Ranch & Lodge

The Sierra Diablo Ranch & Lodge is a working ranch. The innkeeper invites you to experience a uniquely western adventure by joining one of the ranch's cattle drives, which take place three times a year. This is a week-long process as they drive the cattle to the ranch, brand them and work the cows and calves. Call ahead as space is limited and these weeks are very popular.

The Sierra Diablo "brings you the Old West ranch experience in style!"

INNKEEPERS:	Woodrow & Sandra Bean
ADDRESS:	2.8 Miles Northeast of Sierra Blanca
	Sierra Blanca, Texas 79851
TELEPHONE:	(915) 986-2502; (800) 986-9940
E-MAIL:	ranch@sierradiablo.com
WEBSITE:	www.sierradiablo.com
ROOMS:	5 Rooms; 1 Suite; Private & shared baths
CHILDREN:	Children age 16 and older welcome
ANIMALS:	Not allowed
HANDICAPPED:	Not handicapped accessible
DIETARY NEEDS:	Will accommodate guests' special dietary needs

Down-Home Chicken Fried Steak with Cream Gravy

Makes 6 Servings

"A melt-in-your-mouth steak. Buttermilk and olive oil are the key ingredients."
- Innkeeper, Sierra Diablo Ranch & Lodge. Note: the steaks need to soak
overnight in the buttermilk.

6	(½-inch thick) rib eye steaks
1	quart buttermilk
3-4	cups olive oil

Salt and pepper, to taste

4	cups flour

Cream gravy:

¼	cup olive oil (reserved from cooking steaks)
3	tablespoons flour
3	cups (about) milk

Salt and pepper, to taste

Soak the steaks in the buttermilk overnight, refrigerated, in a large covered bowl or other suitable container.

The next day, heat olive oil in a large cast-iron skillet over medium-high heat. Remove steaks from buttermilk, reserving buttermilk in bowl. Season steaks with salt and pepper, then dip each in flour to coat both sides. Re-dip in buttermilk and coat with flour a second time.

Cook steaks in hot oil until browned on both sides and cooked to desired temperature. Drain steaks on paper towels (reserve ¼ cup of the cooking oil for the gravy), then stack on a serving platter. Serve with cream gravy. Mmm-good!

For the cream gravy: Put the reserved ¼ cup of steak cooking oil in a skillet. Add 3 tablespoons flour. Whisk until well blended. Slowly add enough milk to reach desired gravy consistency. Season with salt and pepper.

Blair House

B lair House is a respite from today's busy world. A lovely, nine-room inn nestled on 24 acres of gorgeous Texas Hill Country, Blair House offers a healthy dose of southern hospitality and an appealing list of leisure activities, including three nearby golf courses, 125 shops and galleries to visit and the Blanco River, Cypress Creek and Canyon Lake.

"Your romantic inn has exceeded all expectations. Thanks for making our vacation an exceptional experience." ~ Guest, Cleveland, Ohio

INNKEEPERS:	Mike & Vickie Schneider
ADDRESS:	100 Spoke Hill Road
	Wimberley, Texas 78676
TELEPHONE:	(512) 847-1111; (877) 549-5450
E-MAIL:	info@blairhouseinn.com
WEBSITE:	www.blairhouseinn.com
ROOMS:	9 Rooms; Private baths
CHILDREN:	Children age 12 and older welcome
ANIMALS:	Not allowed; Resident dog
HANDICAPPED:	Handicapped accessible
DIETARY NEEDS:	Will accommodate guests' special dietary needs

Chili-Marinated Flank Steak

Makes 6 Servings

½   cup red wine vinegar
⅓   cup olive oil
¼   cup chili powder
2½   tablespoons garlic powder
2½   tablespoons Hungarian sweet paprika
1   tablespoon salt
2   tablespoons packed brown sugar
½   cup chopped red onion
1   large or 2 small bay leaves, crumbled
1   fresh thyme sprig
1   fresh rosemary sprig
1   (2-pound) flank steak
3   cups mesquite chips, soaked in water for 1 hour
Caramelized onions (recipe follows)

Whisk together vinegar, olive oil, chili powder, garlic powder, paprika, salt and brown sugar (the mixture will be thick). Add onion, bay leaves, thyme and rosemary. Put steak in a glass baking dish. Spread ½ of marinade over top of meat. Turn and coat the other side with the remaining marinade. Cover with plastic wrap. Refrigerate for at least 1 day and up to 2 days.

When ready to cook, heat grill to medium-high heat. Drain mesquite chips and sprinkle over coals (or put in a smoker box). Brush grill rack with oil. Scrape almost all of the marinade off the meat; discard marinade. Grill steak to desired doneness, about 4 minutes per side for medium-rare. Transfer steak to a cutting board; let stand for 5 minutes. Slice steak diagonally, across the grain, into very thin slices. Serve with caramelized onions.

Caramelized onions:
2   tablespoons olive oil
2   tablespoons butter
2   onions, thinly sliced into rings
2   teaspoons sugar

Heat olive oil and butter in a skillet over medium to medium-high heat. Add onions; cook until starting to brown, about 5 minutes. Lower heat to medium-low, sprinkle with sugar and cook for 10-15 minutes more, until golden and tender. Season with salt and pepper.

The Woodbine Hotel

The Woodbine Hotel & Restaurant boasts such features as restored native, virgin yellow pine woodwork and original decorative plinth blocks with bluebonnets above each doorway and window. Historically correct wallpaper hangs in each room and beautiful porches wrap around the upstairs and along the front and back of the building.

The Woodbine Hotel was entered into the National Register of Historic Places in 1980 and became a Texas Historic Landmark in 1982.

INNKEEPERS:	Chef Reinhard & Susan Warmuth
ADDRESS:	209 North Madison
	Madisonville, Texas 77864
TELEPHONE:	(936) 348-3333
E-MAIL:	woodbinehotel@aol.com
WEBSITE:	www.woodbinehotel.com
ROOMS:	8 Rooms; Private baths
CHILDREN:	Call ahead
ANIMALS:	Not allowed
HANDICAPPED:	Call ahead
DIETARY NEEDS:	Will accommodate guests' special dietary needs

Pecan-Crusted Boneless Pork Chop with Jack Daniels Single Barrel Bourbon Demi-Glace

Makes 4 Servings

2	shallots
1	sprig fresh rosemary (leaves only)
1	tablespoon fresh thyme
¼	cup olive oil
4	(10-ounce) boneless center cut pork loin chops
¼	cup Jack Daniels Single Barrel Bourbon
¼	cup dry red wine
1	cup demi-glace (homemade or store-bought)
6	ounces pecans
¼	cup pure maple syrup

Salt and pepper, to taste

Chop shallots, rosemary and thyme in a food processor until fine. Heat olive oil in a large skillet. Sear pork chops on both sides until brown on the outside but still rare inside. Remove chops from pan; set aside. Add shallot mixture to pan; cook until shallots are translucent. Deglaze pan with bourbon and red wine. Add demi-glace; cook until smooth. Keep sauce warm.

Preheat oven to 350°F. Process pecans to a medium-fine texture in a food processor. Combine pecans, maple syrup, salt and pepper; mix until pecans are moist and well blended. Top each pork chop with ¼ of pecan mixture; press onto chops until pecans stick and cover entire top of chops. Place chops, pecan crusted-side-up, on a rimmed baking sheet; bake until chops are done and pecans are golden brown, about 15 minutes. Remove chops and mix any cooking liquids from the baking sheet into the sauce.

To serve: Ladle ¼ cup of sauce onto each of 4 platters. Place 1 pork chop on top of sauce. Serve with potato and vegetable of choice.

The Cook's Cottage & Suites

The Cook's Cottage & Suites provides complete privacy, romance and attention to every detail. Located just one block from Fredericksburg's Main Street, this is the perfect setting to celebrate a special occasion, make a wish, take a walk, hold hands and enjoy each other.

"The Cook's Cottage's one-room guesthouse is one of those rare places where you feel like the outside world doesn't exist, let alone matter." ~ *Country Home*

INNKEEPERS:	Patsy Swendson
ADDRESS:	703 West Austin
	Fredericksburg, Texas 78624
TELEPHONE:	(210) 493-5101; (210) 273-6471
E-MAIL:	patsy@aisi.net
WEBSITE:	www.bed-inn-breakfast-tx.com
ROOMS:	3 Rooms; 2 Suites; 1 Cottage; Private baths
CHILDREN:	Not allowed
ANIMALS:	Not allowed
HANDICAPPED:	Not handicapped accessible
DIETARY NEEDS:	Will accommodate guests' special dietary needs

Pan-Fried Pork with Peaches

Makes 4 Servings

"A delightful breakfast or brunch dish that will have your guests in the palm of your hand. The addition of the peaches is a great way to utilize those wonderful Fredericksburg peaches so prevalent and fragrant in the summer months." ~ Innkeeper, The Cook's Cottage & Suites

2	tablespoons flour
	Salt and pepper, to taste
4	(¼-inch thick) pork loin cutlets
3	tablespoons vegetable oil
2	tablespoons sherry
2	green onions, minced
1	tablespoon green peppercorns
¼	cup chicken stock (use up to ½ cup if a thinner sauce is desired)
3	large ripe peaches, peeled and sliced
½	lemon, juiced
	Fresh mint leaves, for garnish
	Spiced apples, for garnish

Combine flour, salt and pepper on a plate. Dredge pork cutlets on both sides in the flour mixture. Heat oil in a large skillet. Quickly fry the pork on both sides, until just cooked through, about 4-6 minutes. Transfer meat to a plate and cover with foil to keep warm.

Deglaze pan with sherry, stirring up any bits that cling to the bottom of the pan. Stir in green onions and green peppercorns; heat through. Add ¼ cup chicken stock and heat rapidly to reduce and slightly thicken. Just before serving, return the meat to the pan. Gently add the peach slices and heat through. Drizzle with the juice from ½ lemon. Serve immediately, garnished with mint leaves and spiced apples.

Hill Country Equestrian Lodge

Hill Country Equestrian Lodge is located on a 100-year-old cattle ranch in the heart of the Texas Hill Country, an area world renowned for its unique natural beauty and pioneer history. Here, trails cross crystal-clear streams and wind through 6,000 acres of rolling hills dotted with live oak, yucca and wildflowers.

White-tail deer, turkey, jack-rabbits and other wildlife are frequently spotted during rides or from your porch.

INNKEEPERS:	Dianne Tobin & Peter Lovett
ADDRESS:	1580 Hay Holler Road
	Bandera, Texas 78003
TELEPHONE:	(830) 796-7950
E-MAIL:	lovettor@aol.com
WEBSITE:	www.hillcountryequestlodge.com
ROOMS:	4 Suites; 4 Cottages; Private baths
CHILDREN:	Welcome
ANIMALS:	Not allowed; Resident dogs, cats & horses
HANDICAPPED:	Handicapped accessible
DIETARY NEEDS:	Will accommodate guests' special dietary needs

Pete's Pasta

Makes 8 Servings

Seafood, sausage and vegetables combine to make a very pretty pasta dish!

1	(16-ounce) roll breakfast sausage
1	pound raw shrimp, peeled, rinsed and drained
1	(6-ounce) can crab meat, undrained
1	(6½-ounce) can chopped clams in clam juice, undrained
1	(12-ounce) bag cherry tomatoes
1	bunch (about 1 pound) fresh broccoli, cut into bite-size pieces
1	cup snow peas
1	yellow bell pepper, cut into strips
1	(8-ounce) package sliced mushrooms
2	tablespoons salt, divided
1	(16-ounce) package angel hair pasta
½	cup olive oil
½	teaspoon chopped crushed garlic
⅔	cup freshly grated Parmesan cheese

In a large skillet, cook sausage until done. Drain on paper towels. Cover with a plate to keep warm. In a large saucepan, combine shrimp, crab, clams and clam juice. Bring to a boil, lower heat and simmer, stirring frequently, until shrimp turn pink and are opaque throughout, about 5 minutes. Remove from heat, cover and set aside.

Combine cherry tomatoes, broccoli, snow peas, yellow bell pepper and mushrooms in a microwave-safe bowl. Cover and microwave for 5 minutes; leave covered and set aside.

Bring 4 quarts of water and 1 tablespoon salt to a boil in a large pot. Add pasta and cook for about 3-4 minutes. Drain pasta and return to pot. Add olive oil, the remaining 1 tablespoon of salt and garlic; toss to combine.

Put ingredients into 8 bowls in the following order: pasta, sausage, vegetables, seafood with juice and Parmesan cheese. Serve immediately.

Ant Street Inn

I n historic Brenham, home to Bluebonnets and Blue Bell Ice Cream, a great old building is seeing its rebirth as a premier historic inn. The Ant Street Inn combines the finest in Deep South hospitality, warmth and elegance with the conveniences and personal service of a first-class hotel.

Relax in rocking chairs on the back balcony overlooking the courtyard, enjoy the many shops, restaurants and night spots in the historic Ant Street area or dine at the Ant Street Inn's Capital Grill.

INNKEEPERS:	Pam & Tommy Traylor
ADDRESS:	107 West Commerce Street
	Brenham, Texas 77833
TELEPHONE:	(979) 836-7393
E-MAIL:	stay@antstreetinn.com
WEBSITE:	www.antstreetinn.com
ROOMS:	14 Rooms; Private baths
CHILDREN:	Children age 12 and older welcome
ANIMALS:	Not allowed
HANDICAPPED:	Handicapped accessible
DIETARY NEEDS:	Will accommodate guests' special dietary needs

Puffed Chicken Alouette

Makes 6 Servings

"This recipe is a quick favorite for family and friends. It has a very elegant presentation and looks much more difficult to prepare than it is." ~ Innkeeper, Ant Street Inn

1 (17-ounce) package frozen puff pastry sheets, thawed
1 (6½-ounce) container Alouette garlic and herb spreadable cheese
6 boneless, skinless chicken breast halves
Salt and pepper, to taste
Egg wash (1 egg beaten with 1 tablespoon water)

Unfold pastry sheets. On a floured surface, roll each sheet into a 12x14-inch rectangle. Cut the first pastry sheet into four 6x7-inch rectangles. Cut the second sheet in half. Cut two 6x7-inch rectangles from ½ of the sheet. Cut 24 thin (about ¼-inch wide) strips from the other ½ of the sheet.

Spread 1/6 of the spreadable cheese onto each chicken breast. Sprinkle with salt and pepper. Place 1 chicken breast, cheese-side-down, onto the center of each 6x7-inch pastry rectangle. Brush water onto the edges of the pastry which extend beyond the chicken. Pull the edges of the pastry up around the chicken, overlapping the edges to secure. Place bundles, seam-side-down, onto a lightly greased baking sheet.

Twist 2 of the ¼-inch strips of dough gently together into a braid. Place lengthwise on a chicken breast bundle, tucking the ends under the bundle. Twist 2 more strips together and place them crosswise across the bundle, tucking the ends under the bundle. Repeat with the remaining strips of dough for each chicken bundle. (If you are not baking the chicken right away, you can cover and refrigerate the bundles for up to 2 hours.)

Preheat oven to 400°F. Brush egg wash over the top and sides of each bundle (this helps the pastries become a beautiful, golden brown). Bake for 25 minutes, or until bundles are golden brown.

The Inn of Many Faces

Located 70 miles north of Dallas, on the Oklahoma border near Lake Texoma, the Inn of Many Faces is not only a great place to relax and rest, but the location also offers easy access to fishing and boating on the lake, several area golf courses, antique and art browsing in downtown Denison and much more.

Spend your afternoons relaxing on the great porch, catching fireflies in the garden or feeding the goldfish in the garden pond.

INNKEEPERS:	Charlie & Gloria Morton
ADDRESS:	412 West Morton Street
	Denison, Texas 75020
TELEPHONE:	(903) 465-4639
E-MAIL:	theinn@texoma.net
WEBSITE:	www.theinnofmanyfaces.com
ROOMS:	4 Rooms; Private baths
CHILDREN:	Children age 11 and older welcome
ANIMALS:	Not allowed
HANDICAPPED:	Not handicapped accessible
DIETARY NEEDS:	Will accommodate guests' special dietary needs

Poppy Seed Chicken in Puff Pastry

Makes 12 Servings

"We serve this dish at luncheons and showers – it always receives rave reviews."
~ Innkeeper, The Inn of Many Faces

2   (10-ounce) packages Pepperidge Farm frozen puff pastry shells
       (12 puff pastry shells total)
4-5 boneless, skinless chicken breast halves, cooked and chopped
1   (26-ounce) can condensed cream of chicken soup
1   (26-ounce) can condensed cream of mushroom soup
24   ounces sour cream
4   tablespoons poppy seeds
1   cup slivered almonds
Fresh parsley, for garnish (optional)

Bake the 12 puff pastry shells according to package directions; set aside.

Preheat oven to 350°F. Spray a 9x13-inch baking dish with nonstick cooking spray. Combine cooked, chopped chicken and both soups in a large bowl; pour into the baking dish. Bake, uncovered, for 50-60 minutes. Add sour cream, poppy seeds and slivered almonds; stir to mix thoroughly. Bake for 15-20 minutes more.

Place a puff pastry shell on each plate; fill with the hot chicken mixture, overflowing the mixture onto the plate. Top with the pastry puff lid. Garnish with parsley, if desired.

Terralak

The Terralak Bed & Breakfast sits on a hillside on several wooded acres overlooking Lake Texoma and its 600-mile shoreline. Breathtaking lake views and a walking path to the lake create a unique lakeside retreat. Outdoor activities abound. Let time take you back. Be a young child again, throwing horseshoes, playing sand volleyball and badminton, daydreaming in a hammock, bird watching, hiking, fishing, horseback riding and more. With just the boating and the lake activities alone, you can fully connect with the spirit of the countryside.

INNKEEPERS:	Kathy Murray
ADDRESS:	2661 Tanglewood Drive
	Pottsboro, Texas 75076
TELEPHONE:	(903) 786-6335
EMAIL:	terralak@aol.com
WEBSITE:	www.terralak.com
ROOMS:	5 Rooms; Private baths
CHILDREN:	Welcome; Call ahead
ANIMALS:	Not allowed
HANDICAPPED:	Not handicapped accessible
DIETARY NEEDS:	Will accommodate guests' special dietary needs

Easy Indoor-Grilled Lemon Sesame Chicken

Makes 4 Servings

"This chicken is wonderful served with stir-fried or grilled veggies and rice." ~ Innkeeper, Terralak Bed & Breakfast

4	boneless, skinless chicken breast halves
1	cup lemon juice
½	cup soy sauce
4	tablespoons sesame seeds

Salt and pepper, to taste

Rinse chicken breasts. Combine lemon juice and soy sauce in a small bowl. Put sesame seeds on a plate. Dip each chicken breast in the soy sauce mixture. Roll chicken in sesame seeds (or sprinkle sesame seeds on chicken and press into both sides of chicken). Season chicken with salt and pepper on both sides.

Grill over medium-high heat on a George Foreman grill (or other indoor kitchen grill) until chicken is no longer pink on the inside.

Green Gables

Located just 30 miles north of San Antonio and 60 miles west of Austin, Green Gables Bed & Breakfast is central to many Texas Hill Country sites and events, and is the perfect jumping-off point for exploring nearby Fredericksburg, Johnson City, Boerne and other Hill Country attractions.

In Anne's Rose Cottage, enjoy a soothing soak in the antique claw-foot tub with special bath amenities by Crabtree & Evelyn, or snuggle up on the loveseat with your special someone in front of the gas log fireplace.

INNKEEPERS:	Glen & Sue McFarlin
ADDRESS:	401 Green Gables
	Blanco, Texas 78606
TELEPHONE:	(830) 833-5931; (888) 833-5931
E-MAIL:	mcfarlin@moment.net
WEBSITE:	www.greengables-tx.com
ROOMS:	1 Suite; 2 Cottages; Private baths
CHILDREN:	Welcome
ANIMALS:	Not allowed; Resident dogs & cats
HANDICAPPED:	Not handicapped accessible
DIETARY NEEDS:	Will accommodate guests' special dietary needs

African Curry

Makes 6 Servings

This wonderful curry dish is a great way to use leftover turkey or chicken. If you prefer, boil fresh poultry until cooked through. Serve over rice.

2   tablespoons butter or oil
1   onion, chopped
2-3 fresh tomatoes, chopped
2   tablespoons curry powder
⅛   teaspoon cayenne pepper
½   teaspoon salt
4   tablespoons flour
2   cups chicken broth
2   cups de-boned, chopped cooked chicken or turkey
Condiments: Shredded coconut, crushed pineapple, chopped hard-boiled
    eggs, chutney, chopped salted peanuts, raisins and chopped tomatoes
Cooked rice, for serving

Gently heat butter or oil in a large pan. Add onion, tomato, curry powder, cayenne and salt; cook until onions are soft. Add flour, stir to coat and cook for 2 minutes more. Add chicken broth and bring to a simmer. Cook until sauce is a medium-thick consistency. Add turkey or chicken; simmer to heat through (if sauce is too thick, add a little more chicken broth or water).

Spoon condiments into small, individual bowls and place on dining table. Put rice into soup or pasta bowls and ladle the curry over the rice. Let guests add their own condiments.

Blair House

Throughout Blair House - A Fine Country Inn, the mood is gracious and serene, the atmosphere light and airy. Each room is individually decorated to create an ambiance of peace and tranquility. Guests at Blair House can come for a weekend cooking class from the inn's acclaimed chef, with each session covering a great cuisine of America or the world.

Blair House chef, Christopher Stonesifer, was voted one of America's Top 25 "Bed & Banquet" Super Chefs by *Condé Nast Traveler.*

INNKEEPERS:	Mike & Vickie Schneider
ADDRESS:	100 Spoke Hill Road
	Wimberley, Texas 78676
TELEPHONE:	(512) 847-1111; (877) 549-5450
E-MAIL:	info@blairhouseinn.com
WEBSITE:	www.blairhouseinn.com
ROOMS:	9 Rooms; Private baths
CHILDREN:	Children age 12 and older welcome
ANIMALS:	Not allowed; Resident dog
HANDICAPPED:	Handicapped accessible
DIETARY NEEDS:	Will accommodate guests' special dietary needs

Guajillo Rubbed, Herb-Smoked Muscovy Duck Breast

Makes 4 Servings

3   guajillo chilies (dark red dried chiles), or dried ancho or poblano chiles
½   cup olive oil
5   cloves garlic
1   tablespoon cumin
⅓   cup kosher salt
1   tablespoon cracked black peppercorns
4   (6-ounce) Muscovy duck breasts (or other thick, fatty-skinned duck breasts)
Large handful of each fresh herb: rosemary, thyme, marjoram, oregano, or other herbs of choice (soak herbs in water for 1 hour before using)

Honey and blackberry coulis [koo-LEE] (a thick, puréed sauce):
¼   cup tequila
1   cup honey
2   pints blackberries

Blend dried chiles, olive oil, garlic, cumin, salt and peppercorns in a blender until smooth. Cut or score diamonds into skin of duck breasts. Rub thoroughly on both sides with chile mixture. Chill breasts for at least 20 minutes, or overnight. Prep a smoker or BBQ grill for indirect heat. Place soaked herbs on coals. Smoke duck breasts in smoker for 20 minutes.

Heat a heavy skillet over medium-high heat. Sear duck breasts skin-side-down in a skillet for 10-15 minutes, until skin is golden and crisp, and fat is rendered. Turn and sear the meat side for 1 minute; remove from heat and let rest for 5 minutes. Slice duck breasts diagonally; keep warm.

While duck is searing, prepare coulis (or prepare coulis ahead and warm before serving). Bring tequila to a boil over medium-high heat; reduce to a glaze (this takes just a few minutes). Add honey and blackberries. Heat for 3-5 minutes, then whirl in a blender until smooth. Press mixture through a sieve; discard seeds. Keep mixture warm. To serve, spread plates with coulis. Put duck slices on top of sauce. Garnish with mint sprigs.

Hill Country Equestrian Lodge

Hill Country Equestrian Lodge features private cabins and luxury suites that provide guests a luxurious sanctuary from the rigors of modern-day life. The cabins are early Texas-style accommodations, built of native limestone and cedar, that echo the homes of the sturdy German and Polish immigrants who settled the region in days gone by.

Cabins feature two bathrooms, sunroom and a living/kitchen/dining room with cathedral ceilings and a 22-foot-tall limestone fireplace.

INNKEEPERS:	Dianne Tobin & Peter Lovett
ADDRESS:	1580 Hay Holler Road
	Bandera, Texas 78003
TELEPHONE:	(830) 796-7950
E-MAIL:	lovettor@aol.com
WEBSITE:	www.hillcountryequestlodge.com
ROOMS:	4 Suites; 4 Cottages; Private baths
CHILDREN:	Welcome
ANIMALS:	Not allowed; Resident dogs, cats & horses
HANDICAPPED:	Handicapped accessible
DIETARY NEEDS:	Will accommodate guests' special dietary needs

Broiled Salmon Fillets

Makes 6 Servings

This broiled salmon is excellent served with rice and steamed asparagus.

2 tablespoons (about) olive oil
6 (4- to 6-ounce) salmon fillets
Juice of ½ lime
1 teaspoon lemon pepper
1 teaspoon BBQ rub or Cajun seasoning
2 teaspoons chopped fresh dill
½ cup crushed Sun Chips (regular flavor)
1½ limes, sliced into wedges, for garnish

Preheat broiler. Cover broiler pan with foil; brush foil lightly with olive oil (reserve the remaining oil for the salmon). Place salmon fillets skin-side-down and sprinkle with juice of ½ lime. Brush fillets with remaining olive oil. Sprinkle fillets with lemon pepper, BBQ rub and dill. Top with crushed Sun Chips.

Broil salmon (with pan in low position, about 6 inches from heat) for about 8 minutes, or until salmon is done and flakes easily with a fork. Garnish each plate with a lime wedge and serve.

Bogart's on the Boulevard

B ogart's on the Boulevard is a stately home that sits proudly on historic Heights Boulevard. The Heights is one of the few neighborhoods in Houston that has preserved much of its historic integrity and charm. The main boulevard is one of the largest esplanades in the city, and has been renovated to preserve the park-like, old-world charm of the community.

Enjoy jogging trails and gazebos along the boulevard as well as nearby eateries and the 19th Street shopping district.

INNKEEPERS:	Dwayne Fuller
ADDRESS:	1536 Heights Boulevard
	Houston, Texas 77008
TELEPHONE:	(713) 802-1281; (713) 864-2500
E-MAIL:	Bogarts@EV1.net
WEBSITE:	www.bogarts.org
ROOMS:	5 Rooms; 1 Suite; Private baths
CHILDREN:	Not allowed
ANIMALS:	Not allowed
HANDICAPPED:	Not handicapped accessible
DIETARY NEEDS:	Will accommodate guests' special dietary needs

Salmon & Delilah Passionata Salad

Makes 10 Servings

This lovely, colorful salad receives "ooh's and aah's" at Bogart's candlelight dinners.

2   sticks (1 cup) unsalted butter
10   (2-ounce) portions boneless, skinless salmon fillet
4   oranges (reserve two, sliced for garnish)
4   blood oranges (reserve two, sliced for garnish)
1   cup Grand Marnier (orange-flavored liqueur)
Salt and pepper, to taste
Honeydew melon, peeled and thinly sliced
Jicama, peeled and cut into matchstick strips

Melt butter in a large skillet over medium-high heat. Brown salmon fillets on both sides in the butter. Lower heat to medium and continue cooking until salmon is cooked through and flakes easily (do not overcook). Remove salmon to a plate; cover with foil to keep warm.

Squeeze the juice of 2 oranges and 2 blood oranges into the skillet, along with the Grand Marnier. Deglaze pan, scraping and loosening any browned bits of salmon. Season with salt and pepper. Raise the heat to medium-high; boil the sauce gently to reduce and thicken somewhat. Arrange the melon and jicama on individual salad plates. Top with the salmon and sauce. Garnish with slices of orange and blood orange. Serve immediately.

Pomegranate House

The two suites and two garden cottages at the Pomegranate House Bed & Breakfast are elegantly Victorian, draped in fine lace and furnished with antiques and fine bedding. Accommodations give you the best of both the past and the present, highlighting pieces from yesterday intermingled with the comforts of today.

Comfort is assured with central heat and air, ceiling fans and private baths. A full gourmet breakfast is served each morning in the dining room.

INNKEEPERS:	Alden & Billie Moore
ADDRESS:	1002 West Pearl Street
	Granbury, Texas 76048
TELEPHONE:	(817) 279-7412
E-MAIL:	Not available
WEBSITE:	www.pomhouse.com
ROOMS:	2 Suites; 2 Cottages; Private baths
CHILDREN:	Children age 12 and older welcome
ANIMALS:	Not allowed; Resident outdoor cat
HANDICAPPED:	Not handicapped accessible
DIETARY NEEDS:	Will accommodate guests' special dietary needs

Shrimp Étouffée

Makes 6 to 8 Servings

Spicy and wonderful – a great Cajun dish served over rice. The directions are for cooking in the microwave, but it can also be cooked on the stove.

1	yellow onion, finely chopped
2	bunches green onions, chopped
1	cup finely chopped celery
1	green bell pepper, finely chopped
4-5	parsley sprigs, chopped
½	teaspoon celery seeds
4-6	tablespoons butter
2	(10¾-ounce) cans cream of mushroom soup
2	(10-ounce) cans Rotel original diced tomatoes with green chiles
2	pounds peeled bite-size shrimp (if using larger shrimp, cut into bite-size pieces)

Cooked rice, for serving

Combine onion, green onion, celery, green pepper, parsley, celery seed and butter in a large, microwave-safe dish. Cover and microwave on high for 15 minutes, stopping and stirring occasionally (or cook on the stove over medium-low heat for 12-15 minutes, until vegetables are tender).

Stir in the soup and tomatoes. Cover and microwave for 10 minutes, stopping and stirring occasionally (or simmer on the stove over low heat for 10 minutes). Stir in the shrimp. Cover and microwave for 10 more minutes (or cook on the stove over medium heat for 5-7 minutes), until shrimp are just done. Serve over rice.

Amelia's Place

In an old factory building constructed in 1924, Amelia's apartment on the third floor is the only existing apartment in downtown Dallas from the 1920's. The six guest rooms are named and decorated in the personal styles of women of all colors who have made profound contributions to Dallas.

Amelia, a feminist from Louisiana who was said to be the best cook in three parishes, offers genuine Southern hospitality.

INNKEEPERS:	Amelia Core Jenkins
ADDRESS:	1775 Young Street
	Dallas, Texas 75201
TELEPHONE:	(214) 651-1775; (888) 651-1775
E-MAIL:	ameliaj@flash.net
WEBSITE:	www.ameliasplace.com
ROOMS:	6 Rooms; Private & shared baths
CHILDREN:	Children age 14 and older welcome
ANIMALS:	Not allowed
HANDICAPPED:	Not handicapped accessible
DIETARY NEEDS:	Will accommodate guests' special dietary needs

Shrimp Bogue Falaya

Makes 8 Servings

"This dish is named for a river in southeast Louisiana that flows into Lake Ponchartrain. An Indian name, Bogue Falaya means 'singing waters,'" ~ Innkeeper, Amelia's Place Bed & Breakfast

1½	cups uncooked long-grain white rice (do not use instant rice)
1½	teaspoons salt
3	cups water
2	large ribs celery, sliced crosswise into ⅓-inch crescents
8	ounces whole mushrooms, sliced top to bottom into ⅓-inch slices
2	bunches green onions (white and green parts), sliced into ⅓-inch pieces
2	tablespoons soy sauce
5	chicken bouillon cubes
1	stick (½ cup) butter
1	pound fresh, peeled medium-to-large shrimp
2	teaspoons freshly ground pepper

Put rice in a medium saucepan. Add salt and 3 cups of water. Bring to a boil over medium-high heat. Reduce heat to a low simmer, cover and cook for 18 minutes, or until done. Remove from heat and let stand, covered, for 5-6 minutes. Fluff rice with a fork to keep grains from sticking together.

While rice is cooking, prepare vegetables. Put 1 cup water in a small saucepan. Add soy sauce and bouillon. Simmer over medium-low heat until bouillon dissolves (help by mashing bouillon with the back of a spoon). Remove from heat; set aside.

In a large skillet, melt butter over medium heat. Cook celery, mushrooms and onions until mushrooms have wilted. Add shrimp and soy mixture. Cook, stirring constantly, until shrimp turn pink. Remove from heat; add the cooked rice and toss lightly to blend. Stir in the pepper.

Preheat oven to 350°F. Spray the bottom and sides of a large baking dish (such as a 2½-quart deep baking dish or a 9x13-inch baking pan) with nonstick cooking spray. Put the rice/shrimp mixture into the baking dish and bake, covered, for 30 minutes. Serve at once (or lower oven temperature to 180°F and hold for up to an hour or so.)

Ocean House

The Ocean House is so much more than what you would expect in a bed and breakfast. It's an 8,000-square-foot, magnificent, contemporary, Mediterranean-style home (the main house was built in 1936), with a wine cellar a Master Sommelier would approve of, plus a gorgeous tropical garden and pool area.

The Island Fun Package will have you ready for a day at the beach – a picnic basket is packed with food and drink, blankets, towels and even sunscreen!

INNKEEPERS:	Bob & Dahlia Schulte
ADDRESS:	3275 Ocean Drive
	Corpus Christi, Texas 78404
TELEPHONE:	(361) 882-9500
E-MAIL:	bobordahlia@oceansuites.com
WEBSITE:	www.oceansuites.com
ROOMS:	5 Suites; Private baths
CHILDREN:	Call ahead
ANIMALS:	Not allowed; Resident outdoor cat
HANDICAPPED:	Not handicapped accessible
DIETARY NEEDS:	Will accommodate guests' special dietary needs

Ocean House Shrimp

Makes 8 Entrée Servings or 16 Appetizer Servings

"Your guests will love this typical Texas taste. If you prefer a spicier flavor, just increase the amount of serrano pepper!" ~ Innkeeper, Ocean House

3	pounds large or extra-large shrimp, peeled and deveined
	Kosher salt and black pepper, to taste
½	stick (¼ cup) butter
8	serrano chile peppers, chopped (with seeds)
¼	cup chopped red bell pepper
¼	cup chopped onion
2	tablespoons minced fresh garlic
½	cup chopped fresh parsley
½	cup chopped fresh cilantro
2	leaves fresh basil, chopped
¼	cup chardonnay wine (or other dry white wine)
	Juice of 1 lemon

Sprinkle the shrimp with salt and pepper; set aside. Melt the butter in a large skillet over medium heat. Add serrano peppers, red bell pepper, onion, garlic, parsley, cilantro and basil; cook for 2 minutes. Increase heat to medium-high; add shrimp and wine. Cook for 4-5 minutes more, or until the shrimp turn pink and are opaque throughout. Drizzle with fresh lemon juice and serve.

Pomegranate House

Named for the innkeeper's first granddaughter, Zoe Camille, Camille's Cottage is situated in the inn's beautiful garden and pond area, creating a courtyard effect. Decorated in soft pinks, the cottage is perfect for a romantic honeymoon or getaway. A four-poster bed, with crocheted canopy and several beautiful antique pieces, complete the decor. Moonlight shines through dormer windows, creating a very romantic setting. The large bath includes a whirlpool tub, antique hand-painted vanity and a Tiffany light over the tub. Cherubs and roses add a special touch to the room.

INNKEEPERS:	Alden & Billie Moore
ADDRESS:	1002 West Pearl Street
	Granbury, Texas 76048
TELEPHONE:	(817) 279-7412
E-MAIL:	Not available
WEBSITE:	www.pomhouse.com
ROOMS:	2 Suites; 2 Cottages; Private baths
CHILDREN:	Children age 12 and older welcome
ANIMALS:	Not allowed; Resident outdoor cat
HANDICAPPED:	Not handicapped accessible
DIETARY NEEDS:	Will accommodate guests' special dietary needs

Shrimp Fajitas

Makes 8 Servings

This wonderful recipe combines sautéed shrimp with homemade pico de gallo. Serve the hot, flavorful mixture in flour tortillas with rice, refried beans and guacamole on the side. Ole!

1   stick (½ cup) butter
2   cloves garlic, finely chopped
1½   pounds fresh jumbo shrimp, peeled
¼   cup dry white wine
Pico de gallo (recipe follows)
1½   teaspoons seasoning salt, or to taste
Flour tortillas, for serving

Melt butter in a large skillet over medium-low heat. Add garlic and cook just until it starts to brown. Add shrimp and cook until pink. Add white wine, bring to a boil, lower heat and simmer for 3-4 minutes. Add pico de gallo and seasoning salt. Serve the shrimp mixture in warmed flour tortillas.

Pico de gallo:
1   green onion, chopped
1   jalapeño pepper, chopped (with seeds)
¼   cup chopped fresh cilantro
1½   cups diced tomato (about 2-3 medium tomatoes)
1   tablespoon Italian dressing
1   teaspoon seasoning salt, or to taste

Combine green onion, jalapeño, cilantro and tomatoes in a medium bowl. Mix well. Stir in Italian dressing and seasoning salt.

B & B Potpourri

B&B
Potpourri

Bogart's on the Boulevard

Guests seem to love the flamboyant decor of Bogart's on the Boulevard. It has been described as French Creole with a Caribbean influence. From ornate chandeliers and antiques to the fabulous Egyptian party room, there is a surprise around every corner. The grounds are landscaped with equal attention to detail.

A beautiful stone fish pond bubbles in the front of the house, while a full-service salon, spa and crystal blue pool adjoin in the back.

INNKEEPERS:	Dwayne Fuller
ADDRESS:	1536 Heights Boulevard
	Houston, Texas 77008
TELEPHONE:	(713) 802-1281; (713) 864-2500
E-MAIL:	Bogarts@EV1.net
WEBSITE:	www.bogarts.org
ROOMS:	5 Rooms; 1 Suite; Private baths
CHILDREN:	Not allowed
ANIMALS:	Not allowed
HANDICAPPED:	Not handicapped accessible
DIETARY NEEDS:	Will accommodate guests' special dietary needs

Artichoke & Spinach Queso

Makes 4 Cups (Serves 20-25)

"This is a very popular item on our reception menus. Guests always love it and request the recipe. It has a lot of ingredients, but it is very easy to prepare."
~ Catering & Special Events Director, Bogart's on the Boulevard

2	tablespoons oil
1	(4-ounce) can chopped green chilies
2	fresh jalapeño peppers, seeded and chopped
1	cup chopped onion
4	garlic cloves, minced
1	(14½-ounce) can chopped tomatoes with garlic
1	(10-ounce) package frozen chopped spinach, thawed and squeezed dry
1	(14½-ounce) can artichoke hearts, drained and chopped
1	tablespoon red wine vinegar
1	(8-ounce) package cream cheese
2	cups (8 ounces) grated Monterey Jack cheese
1¼	cups half & half
½	teaspoon granulated garlic powder
¼	teaspoon cumin
1	tablespoon taco seasoning
2	dashes hot pepper sauce
1	teaspoon salt, or more to taste
½	teaspoon black pepper

Tortilla chips, for serving

Heat oil in a large saucepan over medium heat. Add green chilies, jalapeños, onion and garlic; cook until soft. Remove from heat. Add the remaining ingredients (except the tortilla chips) and mix well. Return to medium to medium-low heat and cook mixture for 25 minutes, stirring frequently, until hot and bubbly. Serve the dip hot with tortilla chips. Refrigerate leftovers.

Note: *Texas Bed & Breakfast Cookbook* taste-testers also liked this dip cold as a spread on crackers.

Rockin River Inn

The Lowrance family built their Spanish-style home in 1882 on a high bluff overlooking the Guadalupe River. Legend has it, they chose a sturdy stone structure that would protect them from the Indian attacks that had taken their first two log houses at the same location. The expansion done in 1900 was meant to make the home the finest in eastern Kerr County, and it was. With 4,000-square-feet of living space and 1,000-square-feet of covered arched porches, it remains one of the Hill Country's finest historic homes.

INNKEEPERS:	Betty & Ken Wardlaw
ADDRESS:	106 Skyline Road
	Center Point, Texas 78010
TELEPHONE:	(830) 634-7043; (866) 424-0576
E-MAIL:	relax@rockinriverinn.com
WEBSITE:	www.rockinriverinn.com
ROOMS:	3 Rooms; 1 Suite; Private baths
CHILDREN:	Welcome
ANIMALS:	Not allowed; Resident dog
HANDICAPPED:	Not handicapped accessible
DIETARY NEEDS:	Will accommodate guests' special dietary needs

Betty's Apple Salsa Dip

Makes 4½ Cups (enough for a group of 30 or more)

Start this recipe about two weeks in advance so you have plenty of time to make the candied jalapeños – a very simple process.

2	cups sour cream
1	(8-ounce) package Neufchâtel cheese, room temperature
½	teaspoon salt
1½	tablespoons apple cider vinegar
½	cup apple jelly
1	tart apple (such as Granny Smith), finely chopped
⅔	cup finely chopped candied jalapeños (recipe follows)

Apple slices and/or tortilla chips, for serving

In a medium bowl, beat sour cream and Neufchâtel cheese on high speed until creamy. Add salt, vinegar and jelly. Beat until smooth. Stir in chopped apple and candied jalapeños.

Chill for at least 1 hour before serving. (This dip may be made in advance and will keep in the refrigerator for several days.) Serve with apple slices and/or tortilla chips.

Candied jalapeños:
1   (12-ounce) jar pickled jalapeños
Sugar, enough to fill jar of pickled jalapeños 3 times

Drain the liquid from the jar of pickled jalapeños, leaving the peppers in the jar. Fill the jar with sugar. Put the lid on and let the peppers stand at room temperature until the sugar turns to syrup (this can take a few days). Drain the liquid and refill the jar with sugar. Let stand again, covered, until a syrup is formed. Drain liquid again and refill with sugar. Let stand again, covered, until a syrup is formed. When the sugar turns to syrup for the third time, the peppers are candied (sometimes the last sugar addition takes longer to turn to syrup; if this happens, add a few drops of vinegar or water to help the process along). Drain the peppers and they are ready to use.

The Garden Inn

Nestled among palm and oak trees in the heart of the residential area of the East End Historical District on lovely Galveston Island, the Garden Inn offers unique lodgings in a relaxed setting. The inn is ideally located near the Seawall, the Historic Strand and the Post Office Street shopping and entertainment districts.

"I tell guests, 'we specialize in cholesterol.'" ~ Innkeeper, The Garden Inn

INNKEEPERS:	Pam & Mike Gilbert
ADDRESS:	1601 Ball Avenue
	Galveston, Texas 77550
TELEPHONE:	(409) 770-0592; (888) 770-7298
E-MAIL:	thegardeninn1601@aol.com
WEBSITE:	www.galveston.com/gardeninn
ROOMS:	2 Rooms; 1 Suite; Private baths
CHILDREN:	Children age 12 and older welcome
ANIMALS:	Not allowed
HANDICAPPED:	Not handicapped accessible
DIETARY NEEDS:	Will accommodate guests' special dietary needs

Curry Dip

Makes 1½ Cups

"This dip is very popular at brunches and cocktail parties." ~ Innkeeper, The Garden Inn

1 cup mayonnaise (do not use low-fat or salad dressing)
3 tablespoons ketchup
1 tablespoon Worcestershire sauce
1 teaspoon curry powder
1 teaspoon onion juice*
Hot sauce (such as Tabasco), a few drops, or to taste
Salt and pepper, to taste
Raw vegetables of choice, crackers, chips or pita bread for serving

Combine mayonnaise, ketchup, Worcestershire sauce, curry powder, onion juice, hot sauce, salt and pepper in a medium bowl; stir until smooth. Cover and refrigerate. For full flavor development, chill for 2-3 hours before serving. Serve with your choice of fresh raw vegetables, crackers, chips or pita wedges.

*Bottled onion juice can be found in the baking/spice aisle of the grocery store. You can also make your own onion juice by "squeezing" an onion over a lemon juicer.

Beaumont Ranch

A t the Beaumont Ranch, trail rides are true to the Spirit of Texas. With seven miles of ranch roads and hilly landscapes with beautiful vistas, each ride is an experience you will cherish and enjoy. The horses are hand-selected and trained on the ranch with enough spirit to provide a real riding experience but gentle enough for complete beginners.

The Beaumont Ranch is comprised of 3,200 acres of beautiful rolling hills, ponds and wildlife.

INNKEEPERS:	Ron & Linda Beaumont
ADDRESS:	10736 CR 102
	Grandview, Texas 76050
TELEPHONE:	(888) 864-6935
E-MAIL:	spa@beaumontranch.com
WEBSITE:	www.beaumontranch.com
ROOMS:	17 Rooms; Private & shared baths
CHILDREN:	Welcome
ANIMALS:	Dogs on leash; Resident horses & cats
HANDICAPPED:	Not handicapped accessible
DIETARY NEEDS:	Will accommodate guests' special dietary needs

Marshmallow Dip for Fruit Tray

Makes 10 to 12 Servings

For a beautiful presentation, surround the dip with an assortment of colorful, seasonal fresh fruit on a silver tray. Some fruits to consider: pineapple chunks, green and purple grapes, strawberries, thick banana slices, kiwi chunks, seedless orange segments, tart apple slices and mango cubes. Be sure to offer toothpicks for ease of spearing and eating.

1   (8-ounce) package cream cheese, room temperature
1   (14-ounce) jar marshmallow crème (marshmallow fluff)

Combine softened cream cheese and marshmallow crème in a medium bowl. Beat on low speed with a mixer until smooth and well-combined. Cover and chill until ready to serve.

Note: To help prevent sticking, spray a rubber spatula lightly with nonstick cooking spray before removing marshmallow crème from the jar.

The Texas White House

W hether it's the culture of the Kimbell, the Amon Carter, the Bass Performance Hall and the Cowgirl Hall of Fame, or the nightlife of Sundance Square and the Stockyards, the Texas White House Bed & Breakfast – Fort Worth's premier bed and breakfast – is close-by.

The innkeepers will help honeymooners and guests celebrating anniversaries design their own romance packages, including the finest special occasion suites, breakfast served to your room and horse-drawn carriage rides.

INNKEEPERS:	Jamie & Grover McMains
ADDRESS:	1417 Eighth Avenue
	Fort Worth, Texas 76104
TELEPHONE:	(817) 923-3597; (800) 279-6491
E-MAIL:	txwhitehou@aol.com
WEBSITE:	www.texaswhitehouse.com
ROOMS:	3 Rooms; 2 Suites; Private baths
CHILDREN:	Welcome
ANIMALS:	Call ahead
HANDICAPPED:	Handicapped accessible
DIETARY NEEDS:	Will accommodate guests' special dietary needs

Gourmet Fruit Cream

Makes 1 Cup

Here are two variations of Gourmet Fruit Cream. Use the brown sugar cream with bananas and strawberries, or try the cinnamon-sugar cream with pears or citrus fruits.

Brown sugar cream:

2   tablespoons brown sugar
1   cup sour cream

Cinnamon-sugar cream:

2   tablespoons cinnamon-sugar (5 teaspoons sugar mixed with
     1 teaspoon cinnamon)
1   cup sour cream

Mix the sugar of choice (either brown sugar or cinnamon-sugar) with the sour cream. Stir well to combine. Refrigerate for at least 10 minutes, or up to 1 day. Stir before serving.

Put fruit in individual serving dishes. Spoon a dollop of brown sugar cream or cinnamon-sugar cream over each serving.

Sierra Diablo Ranch & Lodge

The Sierra Diablo Ranch & Lodge provides the highest quality horses for your riding pleasure. A daily morning trail ride is included in your stay. The ranch requires that everyone starts off with a training session conducted by their expert wranglers. The innkeepers wants guests to enjoy their riding experience and safety is the key.

Trail rides take place on the 20-section ranch, with thousands of acres to explore. The terrain varies from open plains to steep hills.

INNKEEPERS:	Woodrow & Sandra Bean
ADDRESS:	2.8 Miles Northeast of Sierra Blanca
	Sierra Blanca, Texas 79851
TELEPHONE:	(915) 986-2502; (800) 986-9940
E-MAIL:	ranch@sierradiablo.com
WEBSITE:	www.sierradiablo.com
ROOMS:	5 Rooms; 1 Suite; Private & shared baths
CHILDREN:	Children age 16 and older welcome
ANIMALS:	Not allowed
HANDICAPPED:	Not handicapped accessible
DIETARY NEEDS:	Will accommodate guests' special dietary needs

Texas Caviar

Makes 12 Servings

"A very unique appetizer — I've never gone wrong with this one." ~ Innkeeper, Sierra Diablo Ranch & Lodge

2	medium tomatoes, peeled, seeded and chopped
1	medium green bell pepper, seeded and chopped
1	bunch green onions, chopped
2	cloves garlic, minced
1	(15-ounce) can black-eyed peas, drained and rinsed
1	(8-ounce) jar medium picante sauce
½	cup chopped fresh cilantro
3	tablespoons lime juice
½	teaspoon salt

Tortilla chips, for serving

Combine all ingredients (except the tortilla chips) in a large bowl; stir well. Cover and chill for at least 8 hours. Serve with tortilla chips.

The Inn at Craig Place

Breakfast at the Inn at Craig Place is a treat to delight all of the senses. A three-course gourmet breakfast is served on the wrap-around porch, in the historic, candle-lit dining room or in your room. A sample menu might include fruit bruschetta and an asparagus omelet with hollandaise sauce, followed by a piece of decadent raspberry cream cheese coffee cake.

In the evening, you will arrive home to find your bed turned down, a bedtime treat, a rose and a chocolate on your pillow to hasten sweet dreams.

INNKEEPERS:	Tamra, Sandy & John Black
ADDRESS:	117 West Craig Place
	San Antonio, Texas 78212
TELEPHONE:	(210) 736-1017; (877) 427-2447
E-MAIL:	stay@craigplace.com
WEBSITE:	www.craigplace.com
ROOMS:	3 Rooms; 1 Suite; Private baths
CHILDREN:	Children age 12 and older welcome
ANIMALS:	Not allowed; Resident cat
HANDICAPPED:	Not handicapped accessible
DIETARY NEEDS:	Will accommodate guests' special dietary needs

Stuffed Edam

Makes 1 Cheese Ball

This appetizer is best if the cheese mixture is made a day in advance for full flavor development. Serve with bagel chips or your favorite multi-grain cracker.

1	whole Edam cheese (about 7 ounces)
¼	cup mayonnaise
2	teaspoons chopped green onion
2	tablespoons white wine
2	teaspoons chopped parsley
1	(8-ounce) package cream cheese
1½	tablespoons lemon juice

Cut a 1½-inch circle from the top of the cheese. Scoop out the center of the cheese, leaving about a ¼-inch shell and the red wax coating intact. Put removed cheese in a food processor. Add mayonnaise, green onion, wine, parsley, cream cheese and lemon juice; process until smooth. Put cheese mixture into a bowl, cover and refrigerate overnight to allow the cheese to mellow.

The next day, spoon the cheese mixture back into the shell and serve.

The Texas White House

The Longhorn Suite at the Texas White House Bed & Breakfast features rustic wood furniture, a leather recliner, a living room with fireplace, VCR, CD player, queen-size bed with sitting area and a two-person Jacuzzi tub.

A breakfast fit for "visiting royalty" is served at the time of your choosing. Complimentary snacks and early coffee service to your room are available.

INNKEEPERS:	Jamie & Grover McMains
ADDRESS:	1417 Eighth Avenue
	Fort Worth, Texas 76104
TELEPHONE:	(817) 923-3597; (800) 279-6491
E-MAIL:	txwhitehou@aol.com
WEBSITE:	www.texaswhitehouse.com
ROOMS:	3 Rooms; 2 Suites; Private baths
CHILDREN:	Welcome
ANIMALS:	Call ahead
HANDICAPPED:	Handicapped accessible
DIETARY NEEDS:	Will accommodate guests' special dietary needs

Pecan-Crusted Sausage Balls

Makes 20 to 24 Appetizers

"A great make-ahead recipe. These appetizers freeze well." ~ Innkeeper, The Texas White House Bed & Breakfast

1 **pound bulk sausage**
2 **cups (8 ounces) pecan pieces**

Preheat oven to 350°F. Toast pecan pieces in the oven for 8-10 minutes, stirring and checking frequently (be careful that they do not burn).

Roll sausage into bite-size balls and coat with toasted pecans. Bake for 25 minutes, or until sausage is completely cooked.

The Queen Anne

Built in 1905, the Queen Anne features original stained-glass windows, 12-foot ceilings, exquisite inlaid wood floors and pocket doors, and has many fine antiques throughout. The inn is ideally located within walking distance of the historic downtown, Galveston Strand shopping area, theaters, many fine and casual restaurants, cruise terminal and beaches.

"Your hospitality is exceeded only by the great food and the fabulous surroundings." ~ Guest, The Queen Anne Bed & Breakfast

INNKEEPERS:	Ron & Jackie Metzger
ADDRESS:	1915 Sealy Avenue
	Galveston, Texas 77550
TELEPHONE:	(409) 763-7088; (800) 472-0930
E-MAIL:	queenanne@ev1.net
WEBSITE:	www.galvestonqueenanne.com
ROOMS:	5 Rooms; 1 Suite; Private baths
CHILDREN:	Children age 12 and older welcome
ANIMALS:	Not allowed
HANDICAPPED:	Not handicapped accessible
DIETARY NEEDS:	Will accommodate guests' special dietary needs

Jezebel Sauce

Makes 3 Cups

This zippy sauce is delicious served over cream cheese as an appetizer with crackers. The sauce also makes a wonderful glaze for ham.

1   (18-ounce) jar pineapple preserves
1   (18-ounce) jar apple jelly
1   (5-ounce) jar prepared yellow mustard
1   (5-ounce) jar prepared horseradish
1   (8-ounce) package cream cheese (block-style, not a tub)
Crackers, for serving

Combine preserves, jelly, mustard and horseradish; mix until smooth. Refrigerate until ready to use.

Put the block of cream cheese on a serving plate. Spoon some of the sauce over the cream cheese. Serve with crackers.

Amelia's Place

Amelia's Place is a welcoming, three-story, warehouse-style loft "deep in the heart of downtown Dallas." Enjoy good conversation, play Amelia's piano, read, play Scrabble or just relax. A block from city hall and the library, two blocks from the original Neiman-Marcus and the convention center, the Dart Trolley-Bus stops at Amelia's corner every 10 minutes.

Guthrie's, a four-star restaurant, is just across the parking lot from Amelia's Place. Tell your friends, invite a friend or just come and have a good time.

INNKEEPERS:	Amelia Core Jenkins
ADDRESS:	1775 Young Street
	Dallas, Texas 75201
TELEPHONE:	(214) 651-1775; (888) 651-1775
E-MAIL:	ameliaj@flash.net
WEBSITE:	www.ameliasplace.com
ROOMS:	6 Rooms; Private & shared baths
CHILDREN:	Children age 14 and older welcome
ANIMALS:	Not allowed
HANDICAPPED:	Not handicapped accessible
DIETARY NEEDS:	Will accommodate guests' special dietary needs

Big Batch Tomato Sauce

Makes 5 Quarts

"This vegetarian sauce is good for lasagna, spaghetti, meat loaf, pasta, pizza and chicken cacciatore. It can be used right away, but it tastes even better the second day. The sauce freezes well and is great to have on hand for a quick meal." ~ Innkeeper, Amelia's Place Bed & Breakfast

½   cup olive oil (or enough to cover bottom of saucepot)
2   large onions, chopped
1   large red or green bell pepper, chopped
Optional ingredients for variety: ½ bunch fresh parsley, 2 thinly sliced
    ribs celery, 2 thinly sliced shallots, 1 bunch sliced green onions
4-6   cloves garlic, chopped
2   cups fresh basil leaves, chopped (or 3 tablespoons dried basil)
5   (28-ounce) cans ready-cut peeled tomatoes
2   (15-ounce) cans tomato sauce
2   (6-ounce) cans tomato paste
2   tablespoons dried oregano
1   tablespoon dried thyme leaves
Freshly ground black pepper (about 30 turns)
1   tablespoon salt, or to taste

Pour the olive oil into a very large saucepot over medium-high heat. Add onions and peppers (and any of the optional ingredients, if using). Cook, stirring frequently, until the onions are translucent. Lower heat to medium and add garlic and fresh basil (if using dried basil, add later with the other dried herbs); cook for about 1 minute. Add tomatoes, tomato sauce and tomato paste; bring to a simmer. Add oregano and thyme, black pepper and salt. Lower heat and simmer gently for 30 minutes. Remove sauce from heat and allow to cool. Refrigerate.

Use the sauce within a day or two, or freeze the sauce in 1-cup, 2-cup or 4-cup portions. When ready to use, thaw frozen sauce in the microwave or put frozen sauce (with a little added water) in a saucepan, covered, over very low heat.

Roadrunner Farm

Roadrunner Farm Bed & Breakfast is an elegant setting for a country-style wedding. Enjoy your rehearsal dinner surrounded by your closest family and friends while watching the sun set behind the trees. You can spend the night before your wedding in one of the farm's lovely rooms and enjoy a leisurely, gourmet breakfast before you prepare for your special day. Have your ceremony under a canopy of live oak trees with their leaves swaying gently in the breeze. Your reception can be in the Limestone house or outside on the beautiful grounds.

INNKEEPERS:	Jan Farris Michie
ADDRESS:	10501 Fincher Road
	Argyle, Texas 76226
TELEPHONE:	(940) 241-3089
E-MAIL:	jan-michie@roadrunnerfarm.com
WEBSITE:	www.roadrunnerfarm.com
ROOMS:	2 Rooms; Private baths
CHILDREN:	Children age 10 and older welcome
ANIMALS:	Not allowed; Resident dog
HANDICAPPED:	Not handicapped accessible
DIETARY NEEDS:	Will accommodate guests' special dietary needs

Quick Tomato Basil Bisque

Makes 6 Cups

"I serve this soup with fruit or a salad and homemade bread." ~ Innkeeper, Roadrunner Farm

2	(10¾-ounce) cans undiluted Campbell's Healthy Request tomato soup
1	(14½-ounce) can Hunt's diced tomatoes with roasted garlic, chopped finer
2½	cups buttermilk
½	cup chopped fresh basil
½	teaspoon coarsely ground black pepper

Sour cream, for garnish
Fresh basil sprigs, for garnish

Combine tomato soup, diced tomatoes, buttermilk, basil and black pepper in a large saucepan. Heat over medium heat, stirring occasionally, for 6-8 minutes, or until soup is very hot (do not boil).

Ladle soup into bowls. Garnish each serving with a dollop of sour cream and a fresh basil sprig.

Rockin River Inn

The Rockin River Inn is located on the Guadalupe River, central to the Texas Hill Country. The inn is surrounded by Hill Country native landscapes that display a Texas wildflower show in spring and a spectacular changing of the leaves in fall.

Rockin River guests can enjoy tubing, kayaking, canoeing, biking, antiquing, motorcycling, museums, wineries, bird watching, hunting, fishing, star gazing, Lost Maples Wilderness Area, Sea World, the Alamo and more!

INNKEEPERS:	Betty & Ken Wardlaw
ADDRESS:	106 Skyline Road
	Center Point, Texas 78010
TELEPHONE:	(830) 634-7043; (866) 424-0576
E-MAIL:	relax@rockinriverinn.com
WEBSITE:	www.rockinriverinn.com
ROOMS:	3 Rooms; 1 Suite; Private baths
CHILDREN:	Welcome
ANIMALS:	Not allowed; Resident dog
HANDICAPPED:	Not handicapped accessible
DIETARY NEEDS:	Will accommodate guests' special dietary needs

River-Sitting Sunshine Soup

Makes 8 to 10 Appetizer Servings

"When the river gets low in July and August, we invite guests to sit in the river for afternoon cocktails. A favorite river-sitting cocktail treat is this refreshing, cold soup that's as healthy as the sunshine that sparkles off the Guadalupe River." ~ Innkeeper, Rockin River Inn

1	(64-ounce) bottle Clamato juice
6-8	ounces firm tofu, drained and cut into ⅓-inch cubes
⅓	cup (more or less) finely chopped onion or green onion
2	small-to-medium avocados, cut into ⅓-inch cubes
½	cup chopped celery
1	large cucumber, peeled, seeded and cut into ⅓-inch cubes
6-8	ounces frozen salad shrimp (thaw quickly by rinsing with cold water, drain and pat dry with paper towel)
4	tablespoons red wine vinegar
2	tablespoons extra-virgin olive oil
1-2	teaspoons sugar, to taste

Salt and pepper, to taste

Stir all ingredients together in a very large bowl or container. Cover and refrigerate overnight, or for at least 8 hours.

Serve in wine glasses or clear plastic cups to enjoy the deep red color. Provide spoons for getting out every last bite.

Wisteria Hideaway

Wisteria Hideaway Bed & Breakfast, in the heart of the Piney Woods of Deep East Texas, is a 1939 Colonial-style home that provides an oasis of Southern hospitality and warmth. The majestic splendor of the four-acre Lufkin estate will impress travelers looking for privacy and convenience.

Let the wisteria-laden forests, pine floors and large-columned front porch welcome you comfortably into this grand inn.

INNKEEPERS:	Ron & Brenda A. Cole
ADDRESS:	3458 Ted Trout Drive
	Lufkin, Texas 75904
TELEPHONE:	(936) 875-2914
E-MAIL:	info@wisteriahideaway.com
WEBSITE:	www.wisteriahideaway.com
ROOMS:	2 Rooms; 1 Suite; Private baths
CHILDREN:	Welcome
ANIMALS:	Not allowed; Resident outdoor cat
HANDICAPPED:	Handicapped accessible
DIETARY NEEDS:	Will accommodate guests' special dietary needs

Clear Punch

Makes 5 Cups Punch Concentrate
(enough to make 2½ gallons of punch)

Each 1 cup of punch concentrate makes 2 quarts of punch when mixed with ginger ale. For added color, float an ice ring of mixed fruits or berries in the punch. This punch is perfect for showers, wedding receptions or any type of special celebration. If clear vanilla extract is not available at your grocery, you may find it at cake decorating stores, gourmet groceries, Sam's Club or Costco.

5   cups sugar
2   cups water
1   (1-ounce) bottle almond extract
1   (1-ounce) bottle clear vanilla extract
½   cup lemon juice
Ginger ale (2-10 quarts, depending on amount of punch being made)

Heat sugar and water in a saucepan over medium heat. Cook and stir until sugar is dissolved. Remove from heat; stir in the almond extract, vanilla extract and lemon juice. Cool. (At this point, the concentrate can be divided into 1-cup portions and refrigerated for use within a few days, or frozen for longer storage.)

To make punch, mix 1 cup of concentrate with 2 quarts of ginger ale. Pour into a punch bowl and add an ice ring. To serve, ladle into punch cups.

Ant Street Inn

The 14 guest rooms at the Ant Street Inn have been painstakingly restored by artisans to retain their original flavor while offering the best in modern comfort and convenience. Rooms feature 12-foot ceilings, polished hardwood floors, Oriental rugs and individual climate control. The innkeepers have scoured the country to create a superb collection of American antiques, including the inn's exquisite and romantic beds. Some rooms offer sitting areas, desks, stained-glass windows and two-person tubs, reminiscent of the grand lifestyle of the 1890's.

INNKEEPERS:	Pam & Tommy Traylor
ADDRESS:	107 West Commerce Street
	Brenham, Texas 77833
TELEPHONE:	(979) 836-7393
E-MAIL:	stay@antstreetinn.com
WEBSITE:	www.antstreetinn.com
ROOMS:	14 Rooms; Private baths
CHILDREN:	Children age 12 and older welcome
ANIMALS:	Not allowed
HANDICAPPED:	Handicapped accessible
DIETARY NEEDS:	Will accommodate guests' special dietary needs

Hot Mulled Cider

Makes 8 Servings

"Social time in the winter months at the Ant Street Inn always features this hot apple drink. My husband, Tommy, had a habit of drinking multiple cups of cider, and usually drank most of it before the guests could get any! One time, I thought I could hide the cider from Tommy by heating a percolator of cider inside a storage area. The coffee pot started 'moaning' as some older pots will do. Tommy heard the moaning and thought a guest was having a problem. I had to confess that I was just hiding the cider from him, and he could have one cup."
~ Pam Traylor, Innkeeper, Ant Street Inn

½   cup packed brown sugar
1   teaspoon whole allspice
1   teaspoon whole cloves
¼   teaspoon salt
Dash of ground nutmeg
1   (about 3-inch) cinnamon stick
2   quarts apple cider
Orange wedges, for garnish
Additional whole cloves, for garnish

Put brown sugar, allspice, cloves, salt, nutmeg and cinnamon stick in a piece of cheesecloth or a coffee filter. Tie with a piece of kitchen twine to secure. Pour apple cider in a large saucepan and add the spice "bag." Bring the cider to a boil over medium heat. Lower heat, cover and simmer gently for 20 minutes. Remove the spice bag and discard. Serve the cider in warmed mugs with a clove-studded orange wedge in each cup for garnish.

Note: You can also make this recipe in a clean, large coffee percolator. Put the spices in the coffee filter and fill the percolator with the cider. The percolator keeps the cider warm while serving.

Fruit Specialties & Desserts

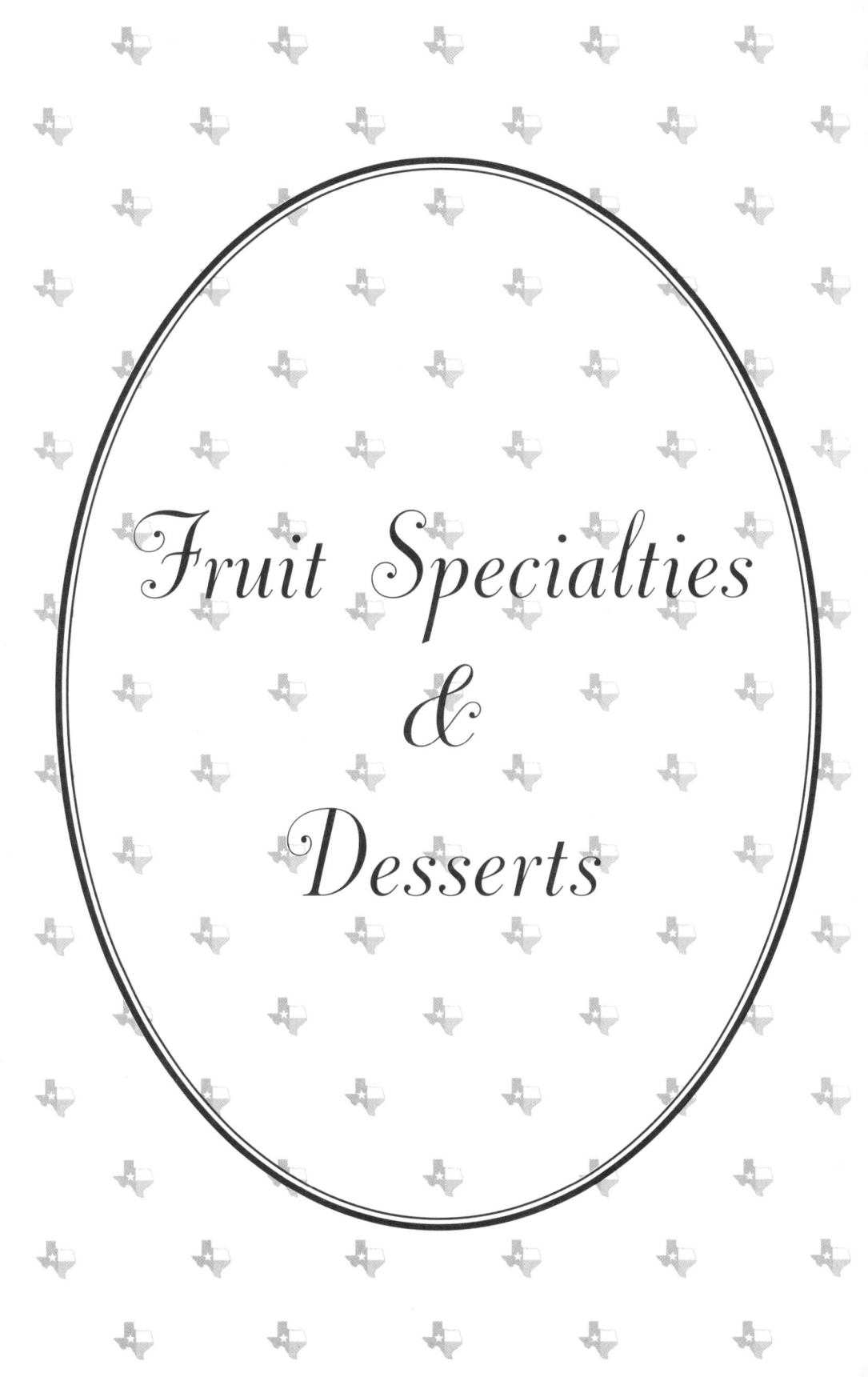

Fruit Specialties & Desserts

Karbach Haus

The Karbach Haus feature four guest rooms in the main house plus two in the newly remodeled Carriage House. Each guest room has its own attached, private tile bath and a sitting area. And each is equipped with cable television, VCR, bath robes, down comforters, designer linens, queen or king-size bed, ceiling fans, antiques and family heirlooms.

The Captain's Quarters has French doors that look out to the side entrance porch, the carriage house and a gigantic cypress tree.

INNKEEPERS:	Kathy & Ben Jack Kinney
ADDRESS:	487 West San Antonio Street
	New Braunfels, Texas 78130
TELEPHONE:	(830) 625-2131; (800) 972-5941
E-MAIL:	khausbnb@aol.com
WEBSITE:	www.karbachhaus.com
ROOMS:	4 Rooms; 2 Suites; Private baths
CHILDREN:	Not allowed
ANIMALS:	Not allowed
HANDICAPPED:	Not handicapped accessible
DIETARY NEEDS:	Will accommodate guests' special dietary needs

Pear Tart

Makes 6 Servings

Pears:

¼   cup sugar
2   tablespoons lemon juice
2   tablespoons pear brandy (or peach or plain brandy)
2   firm, ripe red pears (such as red Bartlett)

Tart:

2   ounces cream cheese, room temperature
½   stick (¼ cup) unsalted butter, room temperature
½   cup flour
¼   cup plus 1½ tablespoons sugar
⅛   teaspoon salt
⅛   teaspoon cinnamon
Powdered sugar, for garnish
Whipped cream, for serving (optional)

For the pears: Combine ¼ cup sugar, lemon juice and brandy in a medium bowl. Cut the pears in half and remove the cores; leave the skin on. Cut the pears into ¼-inch slices and add to the lemon juice mixture; toss gently to coat well. Let sit while preparing the dough.

For the tart: Preheat oven to 350°F. Combine cream cheese and butter; mix well. Add flour, ¼ cup sugar and salt; beat until combined (dough will be sticky.) Spray a 9-inch pie or tart pan with nonstick cooking spray and line the bottom of the pan with an 8-inch round piece of parchment paper. With floured hands, pat the dough to fit the bottom of the pan and up the sides about ½ inch. Prebake the crust for 5 minutes; remove from oven.

Using a strainer, drain the pear slices; discard liquid. Arrange pear slices in the pie pan in a circular pattern, overlapping the slices to fit. Sprinkle pears with the cinnamon and 1½ tablespoons of sugar. Bake for 25-30 minutes, or until golden brown. Cut into wedges and dust with powdered sugar just before serving. If desired, top with whipped cream to which a small amount of pear brandy has been added. The tart is good warm or cold.

Elizabeth's Garden

The Stardust Suite at Elizabeth's Garden is a secluded treetop hideaway with its own private deck, large enough to include a swing and dining area. The spacious loft, with its vaulted ceiling, is soft, subdued and serene. Cloaked in mystical blues and gauzy whites, luxury and attention to detail abound. Antiques and vintage lighting enhance without intruding.

An early 19th-century iron bed wears a palate of soft, muted blues, plums and grays, reminiscent of dusk.

INNKEEPERS:	Bob & Patsy Schlieter
ADDRESS:	412 West Austin
	Fredericksburg, Texas 78624
TELEPHONE:	(830) 990-2504
E-MAIL:	eliza@ktc.com
WEBSITE:	www.bbonline.com/tx/elizabeths
ROOMS:	2 Suites; Private baths
CHILDREN:	Not allowed
ANIMALS:	Not allowed
HANDICAPPED:	Not handicapped accessible
DIETARY NEEDS:	Cannot accommodate guests' special dietary needs

Patsy's Practically Perfect Pears

Makes 6 Servings

"This is a hot fruit dish I created for the holidays. This stuff is addictive – a huge favorite with guests at our B&B! Although we serve it for breakfast as a side dish, it is absolutely divine for dessert topped with Blue Bell Homemade Vanilla ice cream" ~ Innkeeper, Elizabeth's Garden Bed & Breakfast

4	large firm ripe pears, peeled and thinly sliced
1	cup (about) dark sweet cherries, canned or frozen (if using canned, use a drained (15-ounce can); if using frozen, use about ½ of a (16-ounce) package, thawed and drained)
½	cup white sugar
1	tablespoon plus ¾ cup flour
¼	teaspoon salt
3	tablespoons cinnamon
¾	cup old-fashioned or quick-cooking rolled oats
¾	cup packed brown sugar
¼	teaspoon baking soda
½	teaspoon baking powder
½	cup chopped pecans or walnuts
1	stick (½ cup) butter, melted

Preheat oven to 350°F. Spray an 8x8-inch glass baking dish with nonstick cooking spray. Combine pears, cherries, white sugar, 1 tablespoon flour, salt and cinnamon; spread evenly into the baking dish.

Combine oats, brown sugar, ¾ cup flour, baking soda, baking powder and nuts. Sprinkle over the fruit mixture in the baking dish. Pour melted butter evenly over all. Bake for 45 minutes, or until the topping is lightly browned and the fruit mixture is bubbling. Serve warm or cold.

Historic Moses Hughes Ranch

1856

Sparkling springs, turquoise skies and star-filled nights set the mood for rest, recreation and romance at the Historic Moses Hughes Ranch. Deep tranquility and natural beauty surround the two-story, native-stone ranch house, nestled among ancient oaks in the heart of the Texas Hill Country.

The ranch is only 17 miles from the beautiful and primitive Colorado Bend State Park, which offers guided tours of Gorman Falls – the tallest waterfall in Texas.

INNKEEPERS:	**Al & Beverly Solomon**
ADDRESS:	7075 West FM 580
	Lampasas, Texas 76550
TELEPHONE:	(512) 556-5923
E-MAIL:	mhrbb@n-link.com
WEBSITE:	www.moseshughesranch.com
ROOMS:	3 Rooms; Private baths
CHILDREN:	Children age 15 and older welcome
ANIMALS:	Not allowed; Resident outdoor cats
HANDICAPPED:	Not handicapped accessible
DIETARY NEEDS:	Will accommodate guests' special dietary needs

Wrapped Baked Pears

Makes 6 Servings

"This is a recipe that makes a grand entrance to the table. We like to serve these baked pears during the Christmas holidays." ~ Innkeeper, Historic Moses Hughes Ranch Bed & Breakfast

½	cup sugar
4	teaspoons cinnamon
½	cup finely chopped nuts
1	(17⅓-ounce) box frozen Pepperidge Farm puff pastry sheets, thawed
6	firm, ripe pears, peeled and cored (but leave pears whole)
2	tablespoons unsalted butter, cut into 6 small pats
1	egg, beaten

Vanilla ice cream, for serving (optional)

Line a baking sheet with parchment paper. In a small bowl, combine sugar, cinnamon and nuts; set aside. On a very well-floured surface, roll out 1 sheet of puff pastry into an 8x24-inch rectangle. Cut into three 8x8-inch squares. Put the squares on the baking sheet. Repeat with the other sheet of puff pastry.

Put 1 peeled and cored pear in the center of each square of pastry. Fill with 1/6 of the cinnamon/sugar mixture (if some spills out, that is fine). Top with a butter pat. Brush edges of pastry lightly with water and bring all sides up to the top of the pear. Gently squeeze, fold and twist the pastry together to seal in the filling and form a bundle. Fan out corners of pastry dough at the top. Repeat with the remaining 5 pears. (At this point, the pear bundles may be covered and refrigerated until ready to bake.)

Preheat oven to 400°F. Lightly brush each wrapped pear completely with beaten egg to glaze (the glaze helps turn the pastry a beautiful golden brown during baking). Bake for 20-25 minutes, or until the pastry is puffed and golden brown. Serve warm. Great with ice cream.

Bogart's on the Boulevard

B ogart's on the Boulevard is a truly beautiful home featuring six palatial guest suites. The home has three floors and is decorated with antiques, eclectic furnishings, crystal chandeliers, stained- and beveled-glass accents, and many unique accessories. Upon arrival, you will be greeted with welcome treats of the host's choice.

Bogart's is a City of Houston Landmark and was included in the National Register of Historic Places in 1984.

INNKEEPERS:	Dwayne Fuller
ADDRESS:	1536 Heights Boulevard
	Houston, Texas 77008
TELEPHONE:	(713) 802-1281; (713) 864-2500
E-MAIL:	Bogarts@EV1.net
WEBSITE:	www.bogarts.org
ROOMS:	5 Rooms; 1 Suite; Private baths
CHILDREN:	Not allowed
ANIMALS:	Not allowed
HANDICAPPED:	Not handicapped accessible
DIETARY NEEDS:	Will accommodate guests' special dietary needs

Peach Sunrise Enchiladas

Makes 10 Servings

"A Tex-Mex/Gulf Coast fusion dish that rocks at breakfast or brunch – a highlight at bridal luncheons." ~ Innkeeper, Bogart's on the Boulevard

2	sticks (1 cup) butter, divided
1	cup honey
2	cups sliced fresh peaches
½	cup packed brown sugar
½	teaspoon cinnamon
½	teaspoon vanilla extract
10	(8-inch) flour tortillas
½	cup sour cream
1	cup (4 ounces) grated cheddar cheese

Powdered sugar, cinnamon, strawberries and blueberries, for garnish

Preheat oven to 375°F. Spray a 9x13-inch baking pan with nonstick cooking spray. Melt 1 stick of butter with the honey in a small saucepan; set aside to cool. Melt the remaining 1 stick of butter in a large saucepan over medium heat. Add the peaches, brown sugar, cinnamon and vanilla. Cook for 5-10 minutes, stirring frequently; set aside to cool.

Spread 1 tablespoon of the cooled butter/honey mixture on each tortilla (reserve the remaining butter/honey mixture). Spoon the peach mixture equally (about 2 large spoonfuls) onto each tortilla. Dollop several small spoonfuls of sour cream onto each tortilla. Roll up the tortillas and place them side-by-side in the pan. Spoon the remaining butter/honey mixture over the tortillas. Sprinkle with cheddar cheese.

Bake for 10-15 minutes. Place 1 enchilada on each of 10 serving plates. Drizzle with the sauce from the baking pan. Sprinkle with powdered sugar and cinnamon. Garnish with strawberries and blueberries.

Das College Haus

Innkeepers Bitsy and Bob Neuser welcome you to Fredericksburg and the historic Das College Haus. Built in 1916, this Victorian home is a beautiful example of turn-of-the-century Greek Revival-style architecture. The house is tastefully appointed with period antiques and furniture.

The Arbor Suite has open-beamed ceilings, cedar walls, beautiful hard wood floors and a romantic king-size canopy bed.

INNKEEPERS:	Bitsy & Bob Neuser
ADDRESS:	106 West College Street
	Fredericksburg, Texas 78624
TELEPHONE:	(800) 654-2802
E-MAIL:	stay@dascollegehaus.com
WEBSITE:	www.dascollegehaus.com
ROOMS:	1 Room; 3 Suites; Private baths
CHILDREN:	Children age 6 and older welcome
ANIMALS:	Not allowed; Resident dog & cats
HANDICAPPED:	Not handicapped accessible
DIETARY NEEDS:	Will accommodate guests' special dietary needs

Fresh Peach Dumplings

Makes 6 Servings

"Fredericksburg is known for its fine peaches. Many people travel far just to pick them themselves." ~ Innkeeper, Das College Haus Bed & Breakfast

Dumplings:
Pastry for 2 (9-inch) pie crusts
6   **fresh peaches, peeled, halved and pitted**
Fresh blueberries
1   **cup sugar**
1   **cup water**
½   **stick (¼ cup) butter, melted**
¼   **teaspoon nutmeg**
¼   **teaspoon cinnamon**

Sauce:
1   **cup powdered sugar**
½   **stick (¼ cup) butter, melted**
Juice and grated zest of 1 lemon

For the dumplings: Preheat oven to 375°F. Butter a 8x8-inch baking dish. Roll each pie pastry out to ⅛-inch thick. Cut three 5-inch squares from each pastry. Put blueberries in the pit hole of each of 6 peach halves. Cover with the other peach halves. Put a "whole" peach onto each pastry square. Fold up pastry sides and wrap entire peach. Press to shape and seal edges. Prick top of dumplings with a fork. Put dumplings close together in the baking dish.

Combine sugar, water, butter, nutmeg and cinnamon; stir until sugar is dissolved; pour over the dumplings. Bake for 40 minutes.

For the sauce: While the dumplings are baking, combine the sauce ingredients in a small bowl; beat until light and fluffy. Spoon the sauce over the warm dumplings to serve.

Old Mulberry Inn

Named for the oldest mulberry tree in Jefferson, and situated on park-like grounds, the Old Mulberry Inn is just a few doors from the home where Lady Bird Johnson lived as a teenager. The inn's extensive landscaping and splendid roses earned Jefferson's coveted "Garden of the Month" award.

"Personal guest attention, together with the unique charm and ambience of the property, combine to make the bed and breakfast experience one unlike any other." ~ American Automobile Association (AAA)

INNKEEPERS:	Donald & Gloria Degn
ADDRESS:	209 Jefferson Street
	Jefferson, Texas 75657
TELEPHONE:	(903) 665-1945; (800) 263-5319
E-MAIL:	mulberry@jeffersontx.com
WEBSITE:	www.oldmulberryinn.com
ROOMS:	5 Rooms; Private baths
CHILDREN:	Children age 15 and older welcome
ANIMALS:	Not allowed
HANDICAPPED:	Not handicapped accessible
DIETARY NEEDS:	Will accommodate guests' special dietary needs

Fresh Plum Kuchen

Makes 8 to 10 Servings

1	stick (½ cup) butter, room temperature
1	cup sugar, divided
2	eggs
¾	teaspoon almond extract
½	teaspoon vanilla extract
1	cup flour
1	teaspoon baking powder
½	teaspoon salt
4-5	large plums, sliced into wedges or 20 small plums, cut in half
1	teaspoon cinnamon
¼	teaspoon nutmeg

Whipped cream, for serving (optional)

Preheat oven to 400°F. Spray a 9- or 10-inch pie plate or round pan with nonstick cooking spray. Cream together butter and ½ cup sugar in a large bowl. Beat in eggs, one at a time. Add almond extract and vanilla extract. Sift together flour, baking powder and salt; add to the butter mixture and blend well. Spread batter into the pan.

Arrange plum slices, slightly overlapping, around the edge of the batter, then arrange the remaining plum slices over center of batter, reversing directions (if using small plum halves, arrange cut-side-down on batter).

Combine remaining ½ cup of sugar, cinnamon and nutmeg; sprinkle over plums and batter. Bake for 30 minutes. Cut into wedges and serve warm. Top with whipped cream, if desired.

Beauregard House

The Hemingway Suite at the Mobil Three Star and AAA Three Diamond Beauregard House is appointed with Oriental silks, Egyptian carpets and original paintings. This room takes you back to an earlier time – the furnishings are English Victorian and the room is decorated in the lavish style of early 20th-century Europe.

While staying in this historic city, visitors have no need for a car – complimentary trolley tickets are provided to Beauregard House guests.

INNKEEPERS:	Lisa & Al Fittipaldi
ADDRESS:	215 Beauregard Street
	San Antonio, Texas 78204
TELEPHONE:	(888) 667-0555
E-MAIL:	info@beauregardhouse.com
WEBSITE:	www.beauregardhouse.com
ROOMS:	6 Rooms; 2 Suites; Private baths
CHILDREN:	Children age 16 and older welcome
ANIMALS:	Not allowed; Resident dog
HANDICAPPED:	Not handicapped accessible
DIETARY NEEDS:	Will accommodate guests' special dietary needs

Strawberry Semifreddo

Makes 6 Servings

Semifreddo in Italian means "half cold." This recipe features toasted blueberry English muffins filled with a partially frozen, sweetened strawberry and whipped cream purée, topped with sliced strawberries and chocolate sauce. "A true culinary delight." ~ Innkeeper, Beauregard House Bed & Breakfast Inn

2	pints fresh strawberries, divided
3	egg whites
1	teaspoon plus 1½ teaspoons vanilla extract
⅓	cup sugar
¾	cup whipped cream
3	tablespoons powdered sugar
1	tablespoon lemon juice
6	blueberry English muffins, cut in half and toasted
6	tablespoons chocolate sauce, for garnish

Purée 1 pint of strawberries in a blender. In a medium bowl, combine strawberry purée, egg whites and 1 teaspoon of vanilla. Beat with a mixer until frothy, about 2 minutes. Gradually beat in sugar. Fold in whipped cream. Freeze mixture for 1 hour.

Slice remaining 1 pint of strawberries. Toss with 1½ teaspoons vanilla, powdered sugar and lemon juice; cover and chill.

To serve, place 1 toasted English muffin bottom half on each of 6 plates. Spoon the strawberry purée mixture into the center of each muffin half. Top with the sliced strawberry mixture. Place the English muffin tops on top at an angle (so your guests can see the berries and the semifreddo). Drizzle 1 tablespoon of chocolate sauce onto each plate for garnish.

Gruene Apple

E scape the pressures of everyday life and relax in the privacy of the Gruene Apple's gracious atmosphere. The inn boasts 14 spectacular theme rooms designed to provide an experience of total luxury. The creations of many artists and craftsmen have made each room a special retreat.

When you awake, make your way to the dining room with its French doors opening to the tile patio, and linger over a gourmet breakfast at which guests are invited to choose from new specialty items everyday.

INNKEEPERS:	Ki, Lloyd & Linda Kleypas
ADDRESS:	1235 Gruene Road
	New Braunfels, Texas 78130
TELEPHONE:	(830) 643-1234
E-MAIL:	grueneappl@aol.com
WEBSITE:	www.grueneapple.com
ROOMS:	14 Rooms; Private baths
CHILDREN:	Children age 12 and older welcome
ANIMALS:	Not allowed; Resident cats
HANDICAPPED:	Handicapped accessible
DIETARY NEEDS:	Will accommodate guests' special dietary needs

Apple Cream Cheese Tart

Makes 12 to 14 Servings

Crust:

1	stick (½ cup) butter, room temperature
⅓	cup sugar
¼	teaspoon vanilla extract
1	cup flour

Filling:

1	(8-ounce) package cream cheese, room temperature
¼	cup plus ⅓ cup sugar
1	egg
½	teaspoon vanilla extract
1½	teaspoons cinnamon
6	cups peeled and sliced Granny Smith apples
¼	cup slivered almonds

For the crust: Preheat oven to 450°F. Cream together butter, ⅓ cup sugar and vanilla in a small bowl. Blend in the flour. Pat dough into the bottom and 1 inch up the sides of an ungreased 10-inch springform pan.

For the filling: Combine cream cheese and ¼ cup of sugar in a small bowl. Add the egg and vanilla; beat until smooth. Pour into the pan. In a large bowl, combine cinnamon and ⅓ cup sugar. Add sliced apples; toss to coat. Arrange apples over cream cheese mixture. Sprinkle with almonds.

Bake for 10 minutes. Lower oven temperature to 400°F and bake for 35 minutes more, or until apples are tender. Let cool in pan on a wire rack. After tart has completely cooled, remove outer rim of springform pan. Store the tart in the refrigerator.

The Wildflower Inn

Located in the heart of charming Cuero, the Wildflower Inn is a lovingly renovated, 1916 two-story home meticulously decorated in antique style. Frequent travelers and occasional guests alike enjoy a comfortable, cozy atmosphere where relaxation is the order of the day.

The Family Suite has a nursery with a Jenny Lind baby bed accented with leopard print bedding. This room will entertain your toddler with its very own playroom, children's antique chaise lounge and overstuffed armchairs.

INNKEEPERS:	Cissi Grant
ADDRESS:	407 East Broadway
	Cuero, Texas 77954
TELEPHONE:	(361) 275-0250; (866) 275-0250
E-MAIL:	cgrant@wildflowerinn-cuero.com
WEBSITE:	www.wildflowerinn-cuero.com
ROOMS:	3 Rooms; 1 Suite; Private baths
CHILDREN:	Welcome
ANIMALS:	Not allowed
HANDICAPPED:	Not handicapped accessible
DIETARY NEEDS:	Will accommodate guests' special dietary needs

Cantaloupe Pie

Makes 1 Pie (6 to 8 Servings)

"This is one of our favorite side dishes. The recipe is from a friend's great-grandmother whose parents were cantaloupe farmers in south Texas." ~ Innkeeper, The Wildflower Inn Bed & Breakfast

½   (3-ounce) package Jello fat-free Americana tapioca pudding mix
1   (8- or 9-inch) shallow pie crust, unbaked
½   large ripe cantaloupe (must have a great aroma)
¼   cup sugar
½   stick (¼ cup) butter, melted
1   teaspoon cinnamon
Vanilla ice cream, for serving (even at breakfast!)

Preheat oven to 350°F. Sprinkle tapioca pudding mix onto the bottom of the unbaked pie crust. Cut cantaloupe into ⅛- to ¼-inch thin slices. Remove the rind (make sure any green part is cut off). Cut the thin slices into bite-size pieces (about 1-2 inches long). Pile cantaloupe pieces on top of tapioca pudding. Sprinkle sugar on top of cantaloupe. Pour melted butter over sugar. Sprinkle with cinnamon.

Bake for 1 hour (if crust starts to get too brown, cover the crust's edges with foil). Enjoy the wonderful aroma while the pie is baking. Serve warm, with a scoop of vanilla ice cream (this pie is also good cold). Refrigerate any leftovers.

Shopping tip: To ensure a great flavor, smell the whole cantaloupe at the stem end for a ripe cantaloupe aroma.

The Inn at Craig Place

The Inn at Craig Place is only minutes from San Antonio attractions including the Alamo, San Antonio Riverwalk, Fort Sam Houston, the Marketplace (Mercado), the Witte Museum, San Antonio Zoo, Botanical Gardens, the Alamodome and the Majestic Theatre.

The Happily Ever After Suite is light and airy with an outdoor garden motif. The softly draped canopy bed satisfies the most romantic of hearts and a sun room welcomes the new day.

INNKEEPERS:	Tamra, Sandy & John Black
ADDRESS:	117 West Craig Place
	San Antonio, Texas 78212
TELEPHONE:	(210) 736-1017; (877) 427-2447
E-MAIL:	stay@craigplace.com
WEBSITE:	www.craigplace.com
ROOMS:	3 Rooms; 1 Suite; Private baths
CHILDREN:	Children age 12 and older welcome
ANIMALS:	Not allowed; Resident cat
HANDICAPPED:	Not handicapped accessible
DIETARY NEEDS:	Will accommodate guests' special dietary needs

Nantucket Cranberry Dessert

Makes 12-16 Servings

Perfect for the holidays ... yet delicious anytime. A sweet, cranberry nut layer is topped with an almond-flavored batter and baked until golden.

1	(12-ounce) bag fresh or frozen cranberries, rinsed with cold water
1½	cups chopped pecans
½	cup plus 1⅓ cups sugar
2	eggs
1⅓	cups sugar
2	sticks (1 cup) butter, melted
1⅓	cups flour
1	teaspoon almond extract

Vanilla ice cream, for serving (optional)

Preheat oven to 350°F. Spray a 9x13-inch baking pan with nonstick cooking spray. Distribute cranberries over the bottom of the pan. Sprinkle pecans over the cranberries. Sprinkle ½ cup sugar over the pecans.

Beat the eggs in a large bowl. Add 1⅓ cups sugar and melted butter; beat until combined. Add flour and almond extract; stir until smooth. Spread the batter evenly over the cranberries and nuts. Bake for 35-45 minutes, until golden brown. Spoon the warm dessert into serving bowls and top with vanilla ice cream, if desired. Or, cool completely and cut into squares or bars – great with tea!

Make-ahead tip: This dessert freezes well for unexpected guests.

Old Mulberry Inn

T he Old Mulberry Inn's well-traveled owners, Donald and Gloria Degn, have created a bed and breakfast that represents the very best of the inns that they themselves have experienced here and abroad. The inn combines the look of the past with the comforts of the present, while reflecting the 19th-century charm of historic Jefferson.

The American Country Room, reflects a patriotic theme inspired by Mary Emmerling's classic book, *American Country*.

INNKEEPERS:	Donald & Gloria Degn
ADDRESS:	209 Jefferson Street
	Jefferson, Texas 75657
TELEPHONE:	(903) 665-1945; (800) 263-5319
E-MAIL:	mulberry@jeffersontx.com
WEBSITE:	www.oldmulberryinn.com
ROOMS:	5 Rooms; Private baths
CHILDREN:	Children age 15 and older welcome
ANIMALS:	Not allowed
HANDICAPPED:	Not handicapped accessible
DIETARY NEEDS:	Will accommodate guests' special dietary needs

East Texas Cowboy Cookies

Makes 6 Dozen Cookies

2	sticks (1 cup) butter, room temperature
½	cup white sugar
1½	cups brown sugar
2	eggs
1½	teaspoons vanilla extract
2	cups flour
½	teaspoon salt
1	teaspoon baking soda
2	cups old-fashioned rolled oats (not quick-cooking oats)
1	(12-ounce) package chocolate chips (about 2 cups)
2	cups shredded coconut

Preheat oven to 350°F. Spray a baking sheet with nonstick cooking spray. Cream together butter, white sugar and brown sugar in a large bowl. Beat in eggs and vanilla. Sift together flour, salt and baking soda; add to butter mixture and blend well. Stir in oats, chocolate chips and coconut; mix well.

Drop dough by rounded tablespoonfuls onto the baking sheet. Bake for 12-15 minutes. Cool on the baking sheet for 1 minute, then remove cookies to a wire rack to finish cooling.

Das Anwesen

Das Anwesen means "estate, or the homeplace" in German. Yet its deeper meaning is a warm invitation to hospitality – "We welcome you to our home." Das Anwesen (Dahs Ahn-va-zen) is a place of quiet elegance and first-class service, and old-fashioned pride in providing both to you.

Breakfast at Das Anwesen recalls past elegance. Every morning, the innkeeper prepares a Hill Country breakfast served in the dining room on antique china, crystal and silver.

INNKEEPERS:	David W. Hartmann
ADDRESS:	360 Millie's Lane
	New Braunfels, Texas 78132
TELEPHONE:	(830) 625-5992; (866) 526-1236
E-MAIL:	dasanwesen@ev1.net
WEBSITE:	www.dasanwesen.com
ROOMS:	2 Rooms; 1 Suite; 1 Cottage; Private & shared baths
CHILDREN:	Children age 12 and older welcome
ANIMALS:	Not allowed; Resident outdoor pets
HANDICAPPED:	Not handicapped accessible
DIETARY NEEDS:	Will accommodate guests' special dietary needs

Lorraine's Coconut Cookies

Makes 4 Dozen Cookies

"My mother always made these at Christmas as a special treat." ~ Innkeeper, Das Anwesen Bed & Breakfast

1	stick (½ cup) butter, room temperature
1½	cups sugar
3	eggs
1	teaspoon vanilla extract
2½	cups flour
1½	teaspoons baking powder
1	cup coconut

Preheat oven to 350°F. Cream together butter and sugar in a large bowl. Add eggs and vanilla; beat well. Sift together flour and baking powder; add to butter mixture and stir well. Stir in coconut.

Drop the dough by rounded teaspoonfuls, about 2 inches apart, onto a lightly greased baking sheet. Bake for 12-15 minutes, or until edges are lightly browned. Transfer cookies to a wire rack and let cool.

Bliss Wood

Spend some time in a peaceful country setting amidst majestic live oaks in your choice of turn-of-the-century Texas homes, completely furnished with antiques of their era … all on the Lehmann Legacy Ranch, a 650-acre working ranch only an hour west of Houston.

Animals abound on the ranch, including horses, Corriente cattle, llamas, camels, miniature donkeys, peacocks and even American bison. Relax with catch-and-release bass fishing in the ranch's stocked lakes.

INNKEEPERS:	Carol Davis
ADDRESS:	13300 Lehmann Legacy Lane
	Cat Spring, Texas 78933
TELEPHONE:	(713) 301-3235; (800) 753-3376
E-MAIL:	carol@blisswood.net
WEBSITE:	www.blisswood.net
ROOMS:	9 Rooms; Private baths
CHILDREN:	Call ahead
ANIMALS:	Call ahead; Resident dogs
HANDICAPPED:	Handicapped accessible
DIETARY NEEDS:	Will accommodate guests' special dietary needs

Alice's Cookie Surprise

Makes 4 to 5 Dozen Cookies

1	stick (½ cup) butter, room temperature
½	cup white sugar
½	cup packed brown sugar
1	egg
½	teaspoon vanilla extract (or more, to your taste)
1¾	cups flour
½	teaspoon salt
½	teaspoon baking soda
½	teaspoon cinnamon (or more, to your taste)
½	cup vegetable oil (such as canola)
2	cups crushed cornflakes
½	cup shredded coconut
½	cup finely chopped pecans

Preheat oven to 325°F. Beat together butter, white sugar and brown sugar in a large bowl until creamy. Add the egg and vanilla; beat well.

Sift together the flour, salt, baking soda and cinnamon. Add the flour mixture alternately with the oil to the butter mixture (start and end with the flour mixture), stirring well after each addition. Stir in the cornflakes, coconut and pecans.

Drop dough by heaping teaspoonfuls, 2 inches apart, onto an ungreased baking sheet. Bake for 8-12 minutes, until the cookies turn golden brown and achieve a moist, yet chewy consistency (these cookies bake quickly, so check for doneness after 8 minutes).

Pomegranate House

Pomegranate House is a uniquely restored, 1906 country Victorian home where guests can relax and enjoy the atmosphere of a bygone era. Surrounded by magnificent live oaks and arrayed with brilliant seasonal flowers, Pomegranate House is the perfect escape from everyday life.

Enjoy a special romantic getaway package in one of the beautiful Victorian guest rooms. Your weekend will include flowers in your room, a carriage ride to the square and two tickets to Granbury Live or Granbury Opera House.

INNKEEPERS:	Alden & Billie Moore
ADDRESS:	1002 West Pearl Street
	Granbury, Texas 76048
TELEPHONE:	(817) 279-7412
E-MAIL:	Not available
WEBSITE:	www.pomhouse.com
ROOMS:	2 Suites; 2 Cottages; Private baths
CHILDREN:	Children age 12 and older welcome
ANIMALS:	Not allowed; Resident outdoor cat
HANDICAPPED:	Not handicapped accessible
DIETARY NEEDS:	Will accommodate guests' special dietary needs

Sweetie Cookies

Makes 6 Dozen Cookies

"These beautiful pink cookies are very popular with our guests. We serve them daily at our B&B." ~ Innkeeper, Pomegranate House Bed & Breakfast

2   sticks (1 cup butter), room temperature
2   cups sugar
3   eggs
2   teaspoons almond extract
4   cups flour
1   tablespoon baking powder
¼   teaspoon cream of tartar
½   teaspoon salt
Red food coloring

Glaze:
1   cup powdered sugar
1   tablespoon plus 2 teaspoons evaporated milk
½   teaspoon almond extract

Cream together butter and sugar in a large bowl. Add eggs, one at a time, mixing after each addition. Stir in almond extract. Sift together flour, baking powder, cream of tartar and salt; add to butter mixture and stir to combine. Add a few drops of red food coloring to the dough and swirl through the mixture (do not overmix to retain a swirled pattern). Cover and chill the dough for at least 1 hour, or until baking.

Preheat oven to 350°F. Roll chilled dough into balls and place 2 inches apart on a greased baking sheet. Flatten balls slightly. Bake for 10 minutes.

While cookies are baking, combine the glaze ingredients in a small bowl. Glaze cookies while warm.

The Governors' Inn

B uilt in 1897, the Governor's Inn is a Neoclassical Victorian that was restored to its former glory in 1993. Each guest room, named for a Texas governor, is furnished with beautiful and tasteful antiques. You will feel like royalty in the comfort and charm of this well-appointed mansion.

Soak in a claw-foot tub in your private bath. Relax in the parlor or on the wrap-around porch. And, there is always Blue Bell ice cream for guests to help themselves to.

INNKEEPERS:	Lisa & Matt Wiedemann
ADDRESS:	611 West 22nd
	Austin, Texas 78705
TELEPHONE:	(512) 477-0711; (800) 871-8908
E-MAIL:	governorsinn@earthlink.net
WEBSITE:	www.austinbedandbreakfast.com
ROOMS:	10 Rooms; Private baths
CHILDREN:	Welcome
ANIMALS:	Welcome in certain rooms
HANDICAPPED:	Call ahead
DIETARY NEEDS:	Will accommodate guests' special dietary needs

Governor's Inn Cranberry & White Chocolate Biscotti

Makes 2 Dozen Biscotti

1	stick (½ cup) butter, room temperature
1½	cups sugar
2	large eggs
½	teaspoon almond extract
2½	cups flour
1	teaspoon baking powder
½	teaspoon salt
1½	cups dried cranberries
1	egg white
6	(1-ounce) squares premium white chocolate (such as Lindt or Baker's)

Preheat oven to 350°F. Line a heavy, large baking sheet with parchment paper. In a large bowl, beat butter, sugar, eggs and almond extract with a mixer until well blended. Whisk together flour, baking powder and salt; stir into butter mixture until well combined. Stir in cranberries.

Divide dough in half. With floured hands, shape each half into a 2½x9½x1-inch long log. Transfer both logs to the baking sheet, spacing evenly (the logs will spread during baking). Whisk egg white in a small bowl until foamy. Brush egg white on top and sides of each log (this aids browning).

Bake for 35 minutes, or until golden brown. Leave logs on baking sheet; cool completely on a wire rack. Transfer logs to a cutting surface. Using a serrated knife, cut logs diagonally into ½-inch thick slices. Arrange slices, cut-side-down, on the baking sheet (without parchment this time). Bake for 10 minutes. Turn biscotti and bake until just beginning to color, about 5 minutes. Transfer biscotti to a wire rack and cool completely.

In a double boiler, over simmering water, melt white chocolate, stirring, until smooth. Using a fork, drizzle melted chocolate over biscotti. Let stand until chocolate sets, about 30 minutes, or refrigerate to speed the process. Store in an airtight container.

Vieh's

The innkeepers at Vieh's Bed & Breakfast also operate Custom Outings, which offers guided adventures in Mexico, including antique shopping in colonial Mexico, birding in the Sierra Madres, butterflying from the high desert to the low coastal plains, palm and plant trips, and general exploring and sea shelling on remote beaches.

Vieh's is a traditional bed and breakfast with genuine Texas hospitality.

INNKEEPERS:	Lana & Charles Vieh
ADDRESS:	18413 Landrum Park Road
	San Benito, Texas 78586
TELEPHONE:	(956) 425-4651
E-MAIL:	viehbb@aol.com
WEBSITE:	www.vieh.com
ROOMS:	4 Rooms; 1 Cottage; Private & shared baths
CHILDREN:	Welcome
ANIMALS:	Welcome; Call ahead; Resident parrots & horses
HANDICAPPED:	Handicapped accessible
DIETARY NEEDS:	Will accommodate guests' special dietary needs

Vieh's Brownies

Makes 9 Brownies

"My grandfather and father owned Vieh's Bakery – 'Makers and bakers of good things to eat' – in Memphis, Tennessee, in the early 1930's. They developed lots of great recipes, such as these brownies, which are great served with the hot fudge sauce and Texas' Blue Bell Ice Cream." ~ Innkeeper, Vieh's Bed & Breakfast

½	cup flour
1	cup sugar
4	tablespoons unsweetened cocoa powder
½	teaspoon salt
¼	cup canola oil
2	eggs
1	teaspoon vanilla extract
½	cup chopped pecans

Hot fudge sauce, for serving (optional) (recipe follows)
Ice cream, for serving (optional)

Preheat oven to 350°F. Butter a 9x9-inch glass baking dish. Sift flour, sugar, cocoa powder and salt into a medium bowl. Add oil, eggs and vanilla; mix well. Stir in pecans. Pour mixture into baking dish.

Bake for 25 minutes, or until a toothpick inserted in the center comes out clean. To slice, dip a knife into a glass of ice water, wipe knife dry and cut. Serve with hot fudge sauce and ice cream, if desired.

Hot fudge sauce:

½	cup unsweetened cocoa powder
2	cups sugar

Pinch of salt

⅔	cup milk
2	tablespoons butter
1	teaspoon vanilla extract

Mix all of the sauce ingredients, except the vanilla, in a heavy, 2-quart saucepan. Bring to a boil over medium heat and let boil, without stirring, for 6 minutes. Remove from heat; stir in vanilla. Serve hot.

Sierra Diablo Ranch & Lodge

The Sierra Diablo Ranch has been in the Bean family for nearly 100 years. The ranch is home to some of the largest mule deer in the "great state of Texas." Antelope, coyotes, desert quail, roadrunners, jack rabbits, prairie dogs and even big horn sheep can be seen in the sprawling hills. The ranch contains over 12,800 acres of prime west Texas cattle country.

The ranch offers horseback riding, afternoon trail rides, cattle drives, trap shooting, hiking and a swimming pool and Jacuzzi.

INNKEEPERS:	Woodrow & Sandra Bean
ADDRESS:	2.8 Miles Northeast of Sierra Blanca
	Sierra Blanca, Texas 79851
TELEPHONE:	(915) 986-2502; (800) 986-9940
E-MAIL:	ranch@sierradiablo.com
WEBSITE:	www.sierradiablo.com
ROOMS:	5 Rooms; 1 Suite; Private & shared baths
CHILDREN:	Children age 16 and older welcome
ANIMALS:	Not allowed
HANDICAPPED:	Not handicapped accessible
DIETARY NEEDS:	Will accommodate guests' special dietary needs

Diablo Chocolate Cake

Makes 16 Servings

"This is a very easy and delicious cake. The recipe has been handed down for years in our family." ~ Innkeeper, Sierra Diablo Ranch & Lodge

2	cups flour
2	cups sugar
1	stick (½ cup) butter
½	cup shortening
1	cup water
3½	tablespoons unsweetened cocoa powder
1	teaspoon vanilla extract
½	cup buttermilk
1	teaspoon baking soda
2	eggs

Chocolate frosting (recipe follows)

Preheat oven to 400°F. Grease and flour a 10x15-inch sheet cake pan. Sift flour and sugar together into a large bowl. In a saucepan, combine butter, shortening, water and cocoa powder. Bring to a boil over medium heat, then pour over the flour and sugar. Beat with a mixer until combined. Add vanilla, buttermilk, baking soda and eggs; beat well. Pour the batter into the pan. Bake for 20 minutes. After the cake has been baking for 15 minutes, start the frosting. Frost the cake while hot. Cool on a wire rack.

Chocolate frosting:

1	stick (½ cup) butter
3½	tablespoons unsweetened cocoa powder
⅓	cup evaporated milk
1	(16-ounce) box powdered sugar
1	cup chopped pecans
1	teaspoon vanilla

Combine butter, cocoa powder and evaporated milk in a saucepan; bring to a boil over medium heat. Remove from heat. Add powdered sugar, pecans and vanilla; stir well.

Ragtime Ranch Inn

Come and enjoy fields of wildflowers in the spring and summer at the Ragtime Ranch Inn. In the fall, come see the leaves turn brilliant colors and cozy up in front of your own fireplace during Elgin's mild winters. You will enjoy the solitude found only in the country.

There's a rocking chair waiting for you at the Ragtime Ranch Inn. The innkeepers can make any occasion special, especially those get-away events such as anniversaries or birthdays, or just as a break from the routine.

INNKEEPERS:	Roberta Butler & Debbie Jameson
ADDRESS:	203 Ragtime Ranch Road
	Elgin, Texas 78621
TELEPHONE:	(512) 285-9599; (800) 800-9743
E-MAIL:	ragtimeinn@earthlink.net
WEBSITE:	www.ragtimeinn.com
ROOMS:	4 Rooms; Private baths
CHILDREN:	Welcome
ANIMALS:	Welcome (even horses!); Resident dogs & cats
HANDICAPPED:	Call ahead
DIETARY NEEDS:	Will accommodate guests' special dietary needs

Bourbon Cake

Makes 12 to 14 Servings

"Ragtime Ranch Inn won first place in the dessert division at the 1999 Elgin Western Days Food Fair for this cake." ~ Innkeeper, Ragtime Ranch Inn

Cake:

½	cup chopped nuts, such as pecans or almonds
1	(18½-ounce) box Duncan Hines Golden Butter cake mix
1	(3.4-ounce) package instant vanilla pudding mix
½	cup bourbon
⅓	cup water
½	cup vegetable oil
4	eggs

Glaze:

¼	cup water
½	stick (¼ cup) butter
½	cup sugar
¼	cup bourbon

For the cake: Preheat oven to 325°F. Grease and flour a 12-cup Bundt pan. Sprinkle the nuts over the bottom of the pan. Combine cake mix, pudding mix, bourbon, water, oil and eggs in large bowl. Mix for 2 minutes with a mixer. Pour batter over the nuts in the pan. Bake for 50-60 minutes, or until a toothpick inserted in the center comes out clean. Let the cake sit in the pan on a wire rack to cool while making the glaze.

For the glaze: Combine glaze ingredients in a medium saucepan. Bring to a boil, lower heat and simmer for 2-3 minutes.

After the cake has cooled for 10 minutes, poke holes in the cake with a toothpick. Pour the warm glaze over the cake; allow the cake to stand for 20-30 minutes for the glaze to soak in. Remove the cake from the pan and finish cooling. Wrap and store the cake in the refrigerator or freezer for 1-2 days before slicing and serving (this improves the flavor).

The Queen Anne

Breakfast at the Queen Anne Bed & Breakfast is a wonderful dining experience served on antique china and accompanied by candlelight and soft music. Guests enjoy a full gourmet breakfast including homemade breads, jams, jellies, praline sauce and many house specialties.

The sideboard in the dining room is laid ready for hot tea any time of the day with select Ashby's teas, fine teacups and a biscuit barrel filled with delicate cookies!

INNKEEPERS:	Ron & Jackie Metzger
ADDRESS:	1915 Sealy Avenue
	Galveston, Texas 77550
TELEPHONE:	(409) 763-7088; (800) 472-0930
E-MAIL:	queenanne@ev1.net
WEBSITE:	www.galvestonqueenanne.com
ROOMS:	5 Rooms; 1 Suite; Private baths
CHILDREN:	Children age 12 and older welcome
ANIMALS:	Not allowed
HANDICAPPED:	Not handicapped accessible
DIETARY NEEDS:	Will accommodate guests' special dietary needs

Lemon Cake

Makes 16 Servings

Be sure to notice that the oven temperature is lowered two times during baking. The cake bakes for a total of 45 minutes.

Cake:
1   box Duncan Hines Lemon Supreme cake mix
¾   cup vegetable oil
1   cup apricot nectar
4   eggs

Glaze:
Juice and grated zest of 2 lemons
2   **cups powdered sugar**

For the cake: Preheat oven to 350°F. Spray a 12-cup Bundt pan or tube pan with nonstick cooking spray. Combine cake mix, oil and apricot nectar in a large bowl; beat well. Add eggs, one at a time, beating after each addition. Pour batter into pan.

Bake for 15 minutes. Lower oven temperature to 325°F and bake for 15 more minutes. Lower oven temperature to 300°F and bake for 15 more minutes. Let cake cool for 20 minutes in the pan on a wire rack.

For the glaze: While the cake is cooling, make the glaze by combining the juice and zest of the lemons with the powdered sugar. Stir until smooth.

Turn the cake out onto a cake plate. Spoon the lemon glaze over the cake while it is still warm. Let cake cool completely before slicing and serving.

Camp David

Come enjoy Historic Fredericksburg at the Camp David Bed & Breakfast. Shop for antiques on Main Street, browse through history at the Nimitz Museum and the National Museum of the Pacific War, bike through the hills, climb Enchanted Rock, dine at a variety of restaurants or just relax.

A full breakfast is served each morning in your cottage, on your porch or, weather permitting, in the courtyard. Breakfast consists of juice, fresh fruit, home-made muffins or breads and a breakfast entrée.

INNKEEPERS:	Molly & Bob Sagebiel
ADDRESS:	708 West Main
	Fredericksburg, Texas 78624
TELEPHONE:	(830) 997-7797
E-MAIL:	cottages@ktc.com
WEBSITE:	www.campdavidbb.com
ROOMS:	1 Suite; 5 Cottages; Private baths
CHILDREN:	Children age 12 and older welcome
ANIMALS:	Not allowed
HANDICAPPED:	Not handicapped accessible
DIETARY NEEDS:	Call ahead

Ann's Luscious Lime Pound Cake

Makes 16 to 24 Servings

"Ann is our daughter. She loves the taste of lime and is partial to white chocolate." - Innkeeper, Camp David Bed & Breakfast

1	cup white chocolate chips (such as Ghirardelli)
2	sticks (1 cup) butter, room temperature
1½	cups sugar
2	teaspoons vanilla extract
3	large or extra-large eggs
3	tablespoons grated lime zest (from about 3 large limes)
2½	cups flour
1	teaspoon baking powder
½	teaspoon salt
1⅓	cups buttermilk
3	tablespoons fresh lime juice
1	cup powdered sugar

Preheat oven to 350°F. Grease and flour four 3¼x6-inch mini-loaf pans or a 12-cup capacity Bundt pan. Put chips in a microwave-safe bowl. Heat for 1 minute in the microwave. Stir, then microwave for 10-20 seconds at a time, stirring and melting until smooth; set aside.

Cream together butter, sugar and vanilla in a large mixing bowl. Beat in eggs, one at a time, beating well after each addition. Beat in lime zest and melted chips. Sift together flour, baking powder and salt. Beat in flour mixture alternately with buttermilk, beginning and ending with the flour mixture, beating well after each addition. Spoon batter into pan(s).

Bake mini-loaves for 25-35 minutes or Bundt cake for 45-55 minutes, or until a toothpick inserted in the center comes out clean. Cool in pan(s) on a wire rack (10 minutes for mini-loaves or 20 minutes for Bundt cake).

Make a glaze by combining lime juice and powdered sugar; stir until smooth. Remove warm cake from pan(s). Poke holes in cake(s) with a toothpick; drizzle with ½ of the glaze. Wait for 5 minutes, then repeat with the remaining glaze. Cool completely before serving. This cake freezes well.

Lazy Oak

A ward-winning restaurants, shopping, hiking and biking trails, and wonderful Town Lake are within walking distance of the Lazy Oak. Other nearby attractions include the University of Texas, Barton Springs Pool, the Wildflower Center and the beautiful Texas Hill Country.

The Lazy Oak provides luxurious amenities in each room, including bath salts, salon shampoos and robes. A hot tub is located on the back deck.

INNKEEPERS:	Renee & Kevin Buck
ADDRESS:	211 West Live Oak Street
	Austin, Texas 78704
TELEPHONE:	(512) 447-8873; (877) 947-8873
E-MAIL:	lazyoakinn@aol.com
WEBSITE:	www.lazyoakbandb.com
ROOMS:	5 Rooms; Private baths
CHILDREN:	Children age 15 and older welcome
ANIMALS:	Not allowed; Resident dog
HANDICAPPED:	Not handicapped accessible
DIETARY NEEDS:	Will accommodate guests' special dietary needs

Grandmother O'Neal's Chocolate Pie

Makes 6 to 8 Servings

"This is my great grandmother's recipe. It is very rich — serve small pieces with whipped cream." ~ Innkeeper, Lazy Oak Bed & Breakfast

1	(9-inch) pie crust, unbaked
1½	cups sugar
3	heaping tablespoons flour
4	tablespoons unsweetened cocoa powder
1	cup milk
4	eggs
1	stick (½ cup) butter
1	teaspoon vanilla extract

Whipped cream, for serving

Preheat oven to 325°F. Partially bake the unfilled pie crust for 10 minutes; set aside to cool.

Combine sugar, flour and cocoa powder in a medium saucepan. Add just enough of the milk to make a paste. Add eggs, one at a time, mixing well after each addition. Stir in remaining milk. Heat mixture over medium-low to medium heat, stirring constantly, until very thick, about 10-12 minutes (the mixture will look like bubbling lava). Remove from heat. Add the butter and vanilla; stir until butter is melted and mixture is well combined and smooth. Pour mixture into cooled pie shell.

Bake for 45-60 minutes. Cool. Serve with whipped cream, if desired. Refrigerate any leftovers.

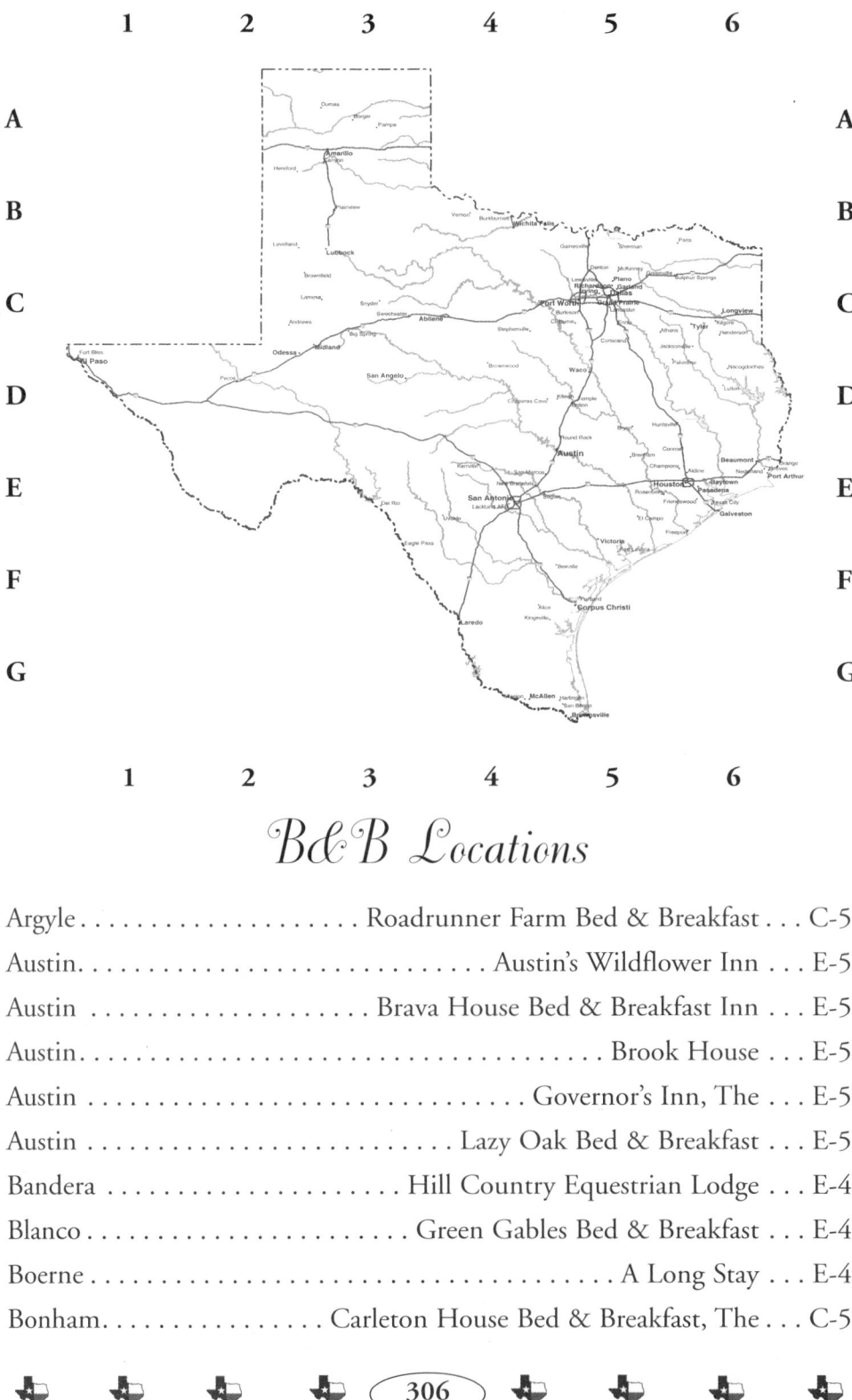

| | 1 | 2 | 3 | 4 | 5 | 6 |

B&B Locations

Alphabetical Listing of B&Bs

Index

About the Authors

Carol McCollum Faino, a graduate of the University of Iowa, former teacher and award-winning author, started cooking as a young girl. Her creative cooking efforts were first publicly recognized when she received the Home Economics Superintendent's Award as a high school senior. She honed her culinary skills attending cooking classes, while raising three children and teaching elementary school. She moved fourteen times in thirty-four years with her husband, a former Navy pilot, having spent more than ten of those years in Texas, including Corpus Christi, El Paso and the Dallas-Fort Worth area. Carol and her husband, Rod, enjoy traveling, seeking out new bed and breakfasts and collecting simple, yet sensational recipes. They currently reside in Castle Rock, Colorado, and have three grown children, Kyle, Erin, Ryan and a daughter-in-law Laura.

Carol is co-author with Doreen Hazledine of the *Colorado Bed & Breakfast Cookbook*, the *Washington State Bed & Breakfast Cookbook*, the *California Wine Country Bed & Breakfast Cookbook and Travel Guide,* and is pleased to have co-authored the latest book in the Bed & Breakfast Cookbook Series™, the *Texas Bed & Breakfast Cookbook*, with her daughter, Erin Faino.

Erin Faino was born in Honolulu, Hawaii. The middle child in a career Navy family, she lived in eight different states growing up. The Lone Star State was "home" four different times, and she graduated from high school in Arlington, Texas. While earning her degree from George Mason University in Virginia, she surrounded herself with top-notch chefs in fine dining establishments in Washington, DC and later Denver, Colorado, working in the restaurant industry. During 10 years in the profession, Erin gleaned a wealth of culinary expertise, and has proven to be a valuable asset to the Bed & Breakfast Cookbook Series™ team. In addition to being a seasoned traveler and an accomplished cook, Erin teaches Special Education in the Richardson Independent School District. She presently resides in Dallas, Texas. The *Texas Bed & Breakfast Cookbook* is Erin's first book.

The Bed & Breakfast Cookbook Series

Entertain with ease and flair! B&B's and Country Inns from across the nation share their best and most requested recipes.

California Bed & Breakfast Cookbook
127 California B&B's and Country Inns. Book #5 in the series.
$19.95 / 328pp / ISBN 1-889593-11-7

Colorado Bed & Breakfast Cookbook
88 Colorado B&B's and Country Inns. Book #1 in the series. New 2nd ed!
$19.95 / 320pp / ISBN 0-9653751-0-2

New England Bed & Breakfast Cookbook
107 B&B's and Country Inns in CT, MA, ME, NH, RI & VT. Book #6.
$19.95 / 320pp / ISBN 1-889593-12-5

North Carolina Bed & Breakfast Cookbook
62 North Carolina B&B's and Country Inns. Book #7 in the series. New!
$19.95 / 320pp / ISBN 1-889593-08-7

Texas Bed & Breakfast Cookbook
70 Texas B&B's, Guest Ranches and Country Inns. Book #3 in the series.
$19.95 / 320pp / ISBN 1-889593-07-9

Virginia Bed & Breakfast Cookbook
94 Virginia B&B's and Country Inns. Book #4 in the series. New 2nd ed.
$19.95 / 320pp / ISBN 1-889593-04-1

Washington State Bed & Breakfast Cookbook
72 Washington B&B's and Country Inns. Book #2 in the series. New 2nd ed!
$19.95 / 320pp / ISBN 1-889593-05-2

✳ Coming Soon: *Georgia, New York & Pennsylvania* (Spring, 2006). ✳

Bed & Breakfast Cookbook Series
Order Form

2969 Baseline Road, Boulder CO 80303
888.456.3607 • www.3dpress.net • orders@3dpress.net

PLEASE SEND ME:	Price	Quantity
CALIFORNIA BED & BREAKFAST COOKBOOK	$19.95	_____
COLORADO BED & BREAKFAST COOKBOOK	$19.95	_____
NEW ENGLAND BED & BREAKFAST COOKBOOK	$19.95	_____
NORTH CAROLINA BED & BREAKFAST COOKBOOK	$19.95	_____
TEXAS BED & BREAKFAST COOKBOOK	$19.95	_____
VIRGINIA BED & BREAKFAST COOKBOOK	$19.95	_____
WASHINGTON STATE BED & BREAKFAST COOKBOOK	$19.95	_____

SUBTOTAL: $ _____

Colorado residents add 3.8% sales tax. Denver residents add 7.2% $ _____

Add $5.00 for shipping for 1st book, add $1 for each additional $ _____

TOTAL ENCLOSED: $ _____

***Special offer: Buy any 2 books in the series and take a 10% discount.
Buy any 4 or more books and take a 25% discount!**

SEND TO:

Name_____

Address _____

City _____ State _____ Zip _____

Phone_____ A gift from: _____

We accept checks, money orders, Visa or Mastercard. Please make checks payable to 3D Press, Inc.

Please charge my ☐ VISA ☐ MASTERCARD

Card Number _____ Expiration Date _____